THROW THEM ALL OUT

THROW THEM ALL OUT

How Politicians and Their Friends
Get Rich off Insider Stock Tips,
Land Deals, and Cronyism
That Would Send the Rest of Us to Prison

PETER SCHWEIZER

MARINER BOOKS
HOUGHTON MIFFLIN HARCOURT
Boston   New York

First Mariner Books edition 2012
Copyright © 2011 by Peter Schweizer

www.hmhbooks.com

Library of Congress Cataloging-in-Publication Data
Schweizer, Peter, date.
Throw them all out: how politicians and their friends get rich
off insider stock tips, land deals, and cronyism that would
send the rest of us to prison / Peter Schweizer.
p. cm.
Includes bibliographical references and index.
ISBN 978-0-547-57314-4   ISBN 978-0-547-97016-5 (pbk.)
1. Political corruption — United States. I. Title.
JK2249.S35 2012
364.1'3230973 — dc23   2011036523

Book design by Melissa Lotfy

Printed in the United States of America
DOC 10 9 8 7 6 5 4 3 2 1

For Maria Duffus—

Thanks so much for encouraging your brother all these years

There is so much honest graft in this big town that they would be fools to go in for dishonest graft.

— GEORGE WASHINGTON PLUNKITT

CONTENTS

Part Three: BREAKING THE BACK OF CRONY CAPITALISM

LIST OF ILLUSTRATIONS

Introduction

THE GOVERNMENT RICH

The mere proposal to set the politician to watch the capitalist has been disturbed by the rather disconcerting discovery that they are both the same man. We are past the point where being a capitalist is the only way of becoming a politician, and we are dangerously near the point where being a politician is much the quickest way of becoming a capitalist. — G. K. CHESTERTON

Just follow the money. — "DEEP THROAT" TO BOB WOODWARD

WE'VE ALL HEARD about the New Rich. Once, they were the Oil Rich. Then they were the Silicon Valley Rich. The Dot-Com Rich. Now it's time to meet the New New Rich: the Government Rich.

For the Government Rich, insider deals, insider trading, and taxpayer money have become a pathway to wealth. They get to walk this exclusive pathway because they get to operate by a different set of rules from the rest of us. And they get to do this while they are working for us, in the name of the "public service."

This is not another book about socioeconomic issues, campaign finance, or political action committees. And it's not about the kind of corrupt politicians who stuff money in their freezers. If anything, corrupt politicians of that sort are vintage stuff now. Dishonest graft is quaint. This is a book about how a Permanent Political Class, composed of politicians and their friends, engages in honest graft. Let's call it crony capitalism. Here the "invisible hand" is often attached to the long arm of Washington. And business is good.

Consider just one example: Dennis Hastert was a jovial ex–high school wrestling coach and member of the Illinois House of Representatives when he was first elected to Congress in 1986. Through hard work, attention to detail, and a knack for coalition building, he rose to be Speaker of the House in 1999 and served until 2007, when he resigned. When Hastert first went to Congress he was a man of relatively modest means. He had a 104-acre farm in Shipman, Illinois, worth between $50,000 and $100,000. His other assets amounted to no more than $170,000. He remained at a similar level until he became Speaker of the House.[1] But by the time he set down the Speaker's gavel, he was substantially better off than when he entered office, with a reported net worth of up to $11 million.

Washington today is full of politicians like Hastert. They have unprecedented opportunities, rich friends, and tight webs of influence. The famous sociologist Max Weber once gave a lecture where he discussed "politics as a calling." He talked about people who would live for politics. But he also pointed out that some people would live *from* it.[2] "Either one lives 'for' politics or one lives 'off' politics . . . He who strives to make politics a permanent source of income lives 'off' politics as a vocation." Today some people are living very well thanks to crony capitalism in Washington.

Politicians have made politics a business. They are increasingly entrepreneurs who use their power, access, and privileged information to generate wealth. And at the same time well-connected financiers and corporate leaders have made a business of politics. They meet together in the nation's capital to form a political caste.

How is it that politicians manage to enter office with relatively meager resources and often retire rich? It's certainly not by clipping coupons or a hefty paycheck. Politicians learned long ago that they could not pay themselves extravagant salaries. People would simply not tolerate it. Back in the spring of 1816, Congress passed a compensation bill that roughly doubled its members' pay. The result? A populist revolt. John Randolph of Roanoke, a Virginia congressman, likened the public's reaction to "the great Leviathan rousing into action." There was universal outrage. As a result, *more than half* the members of the House of Representatives declined to stand for reelection, and only 15 of the 81 who voted for the raise and who did run for reelection managed to keep their seats. Three states—Ohio, Delaware, and Vermont—elected entirely new congressional delegations. Henry Clay managed to retain his seat only after apologizing for voting in favor of the bill and promising he would never do such a thing again. When the new Congress sat, it quickly repealed the act.[3]

Ever since 1816 a large pay raise has been out of the question. In 2011, rank-and-file members of the House and Senate earned salaries of $175,000.[4] If you include their benefits, the pay is more like $285,000 a year, which means they made approximately 3.4 times more than the average full-time worker in America, and twice what private sector workers with master's degrees earn.

That salary makes them the second-highest-paid legislators in the world—Japan is number one. (Luckily for our legislators, their contracts don't include pay based on performance standards.)[5] It's a respectable paycheck, but hardly the kind of money that leads to millions of dollars in savings, especially for men and women who maintain a Washington residence in addition to a house or apartment in their home state.

For many, serving in Congress is the best job they will ever get. Besides the income, they are rewarded with power and responsibility. But increasingly, members are leveraging that power and responsibility to create wealth, too.

Crony capitalism unites these politicians with a certain class of businessmen who act as political entrepreneurs. They make their money from government subsidies, guaranteed loans, grants, and set-asides. They seek to steer the ship of state into profitable seas. Twenty-first-century privateers, they pursue wealth through political pull rather than by producing new products or services. In addition to these political entrepreneurs, big investors turn to lobbying and insider information from their sponsored politicians to make their investment decisions. And business is very good.

Political contacts, inside information, financial connections, and influence are increasingly replacing open competition. Hard work and innovation should be driving the American economy, but in Washington, crony connections have thrown these stable economic helmsmen overboard. Under crony capitalism, access to government officials who can dole out grants, special tax breaks, and subsidies is an alternative path to wealth.

So how does it work?

In his novel *The Reivers*, William Faulkner describes an entrepreneurial scoundrel who uses his mules and plow to make a boggy road even less passable. When the main character's car inevitably gets stuck there, the scoundrel shows up with a mule and offers to pull the car out—for two dollars, a hefty price in 1905. Shift the scene to Washington, and this form of extortion becomes a much bigger profit opportunity. And it's the political class that muddies the road before charging to pull us out.

The new crony capitalists use several kinds of mud. They obtain access to initial public offerings on the stock market that can often be lucrative. They make their investment decisions and trade stock based on what is happening behind closed doors in Washington. This might entail buying or selling stock based on what they know to be going on, or they might "prime the pump," trading stocks based on legislation they have introduced.

Politicians are often extraordinarily good investors—too good to be true. They may not have figured out how to help our economy prosper, but the Permanent Political Class is itself prosperous to a degree that should make us all suspicious. One study used a statistical estimator to determine that members of Congress were "accumulating wealth about 50% faster than expected" compared with other Americans.[6] According to the Center for Responsive Politics in Washington, members saw their net worth soar, on average, an astonishing 84% between 2004 and 2006.[7] (Other Americans didn't do quite so well, averaging about a 20% jump in the same period.)[8] And when times turned lean, in 2009, with the rest of the country mired in recession, members of Congress nonetheless saw their net worth increase by 6%, while the average American's net worth plunged by 22%.[9] Reuters even ran a story on the subject, titled "Get Elected to Congress and Get Rich."[10]

A study in the *Journal of Financial and Quantitative Analysis* found that U.S. senators may have missed their calling: they should all be running hedge funds. How else to explain these results, based on 4,000 stock trades by senators:

- The average American investor underperforms the market.
- The average corporate insider, trading his own company's stock, beats the market by 7% a year.
- The average hedge fund beats the market by between 7% and 8% a year.
- The average senator beats the market by 12% a year.[11]

When the same team looked at 16,000 trades by members of the House of Representatives, they found similar if less spectacular results. House members beat the market by 6% a year, almost as much as what corporate insiders achieve when trading their own stock.[12] (It is unclear why senators are better investors than are representatives. Perhaps it is because they have relatively more power and therefore greater access to market-moving information.)

Another study, by scholars at MIT and Yale, looked at a shorter period of time, from 2004 to 2008, and found that while many individual legislators do not beat the market, they do extremely well with stock in companies with which they are "politically connected." They beat the market by almost 5% a year. As the researchers put it, "Members of Congress seem to benefit as investors from knowledge of companies to which they are politically connected (and particularly those headquartered in their districts), and they appear to take advantage of this knowledge by investing disproportionately in those companies."[13]

"They seem to know something that other people don't know," said Jens Hainmueller, coauthor of the study and an assistant professor of political science at the Massachusetts Institute of Technology.[14]

The winners are the politicians who possess insider knowledge, or who are most likely to receive favors from wealthy supplicants.

That's one side of the crony-capitalist spider web. On the other side are the political entrepreneurs and private investors. There is disturbing evidence that politically connected hedge funds perform dramatically better than those without Washington contacts. One study found that politically connected hedge funds beat their equivalent nonpolitical counterparts by about 2% *per month*.[15]

In short, the Permanent Political Class has clearly figured out how to extract wealth from the rest of us based solely on their position and proximity to power. If you have a seat at the table, you are in for a feast. If you don't have a seat at the table, you are probably on the menu. Exactly how crony capitalists are consuming public wealth and fattening themselves is the subject of this book.

Ideology and political philosophy matter in Washington, but often less than you might think. Honest graft is generally bipartisan. Complex bills that are hundreds or even thousands of pages long can contain a single sentence or word that translates into money and that can influence how a politician votes. One study by scholars at the University of Pennsylvania's Wharton School of Business and the University of Chicago found that during the critical votes on the subprime-mortgage bailout and subsequent matters related to the financial crisis of 2008, a key factor in how members of Congress voted was whether they held stock in banks and in the financial sector. Personal equity ownership also influenced congressional committee decisions on the amount of bailout money particular financial institutions received and how quickly they got it. Apparently the vote had less to do with your politics and more to do with your pocketbook.[16]

Is it any surprise that Washington lawmakers are staying in office longer than they did before, and that in recent years we've had the oldest Congress ever?[17] Long gone are the days when Thomas Jefferson could write, as he did in 1807 to Count Jules Diodati, "I have the consolation of having added nothing to my private fortune during my public service, and of retiring with hands as clean as they are empty."[18] Now, politicians' fortunes are rising, and they are clinging to their jobs for all they're worth.

But hasn't it always been this way? Graft has a long and sordid history in America. In 1789, Alexander Hamilton, the first U.S. secretary of the Treasury, announced plans to pay off both the federal Revolutionary War debt and the debt obligations of the individual states, all at 100%. The deal was preceded by massive insider trading in federal and state government bonds. Members of Congress were among the speculators who traded these bonds, based on advance knowledge of the Treasury's intent. According to Senator William Maclay, Democrat of Pennsylvania, speculators sent people in stagecoaches all over the country to buy up federal and state notes at a fraction of their face value.[19]

Crony capitalism is not new, but it has become a dominant force in Washington. The amount of money to be made is much larger. And the opportunities have become more frequent. In fact, it is now threatening the health and integrity of our entire economic system. "Crony capitalism" is a term that used to be applied almost exclusively to developing countries that were rife with corruption. Now the label can be applied to many sectors of our economy. It is an important part of the reason we face the economic crisis that we do.

One of the best-known chroniclers of crony capitalism in the nineteenth century was one of its participants. George Washington Plunkitt was a party boss of the infamous Tammany Hall, the corrupt political machine that ruled New York City for decades. Plunkitt was born in poverty, in a squatter's hut in what is now Central Park. He left school at the age of eleven and became a multimillionaire through elective office. He explained quite candidly in a series of newspaper interviews in the 1870s how he did it.

Plunkitt's philosophy was that politics is a business. How did he begin his career? "Did I get a book on municipal government . . . ? I wasn't such a fool. What I did was get some marketable goods. What do I mean by marketable goods? Let me tell you: I had a cousin. I went to him and said, 'Tommy, I'm goin' to be a politician, and I want a followin', can I count on you?' He said, 'Sure, George.' That's how I started in business. I got a marketable commodity—one vote."[20]

Plunkitt continued with the classic description that has kept his name alive long after his death:

"There is a distinction between honest graft and dishonest graft. I've made a big fortune out of the game, and I'm getting richer every day, but I've not gone in for dishonest graft—blackmailing gamblers, saloonkeepers, disorderly people, etc.—and neither has any of the men who have made big fortunes in politics. There's an honest graft, and I'm an example of how it works. I might sum up the whole thing by saying: 'I seen opportunities and I took 'em.'"

He goes on: "Just let me explain by examples. My party's in power in the city, and it's going to undertake a lot of public improvements. Well, I'm tipped off, say, that I go to that place and I buy up all the land I can in the neighborhood. Then the board of this or that makes its plan public, and there is a rush to get my land, which nobody cared particular for before. Ain't it perfectly honest to charge a good price and make a profit on my investment and foresight? Of course, it is. Well, that's honest graft."[21]

More recently, Lyndon Johnson, while he served in the House and the Senate, told people to purchase advertising on his Austin radio station, KBTC, in order to get his attention.[22] LBJ also frequently used his power at the Federal Communication Commission to obtain licenses for his radio and television stations and to block competitors from invading his markets in Texas. His company, needless to say, prospered. An initial investment of $17,500 grew into a media empire worth millions.[23]

Or consider the case of the late Congressman Tom Lantos of California. He was one of the most respected representatives and a champion of human rights. But no mention has ever been made of the glaring conflict of interest that was central to his personal financial life. A former economics professor at San Francisco State University, he served in the House for more than twenty-five years. Through much of his later public life, Lantos invested heavily in the stock of a single company. He never worked for the company. Indeed, the company was not even in his district.

When he first went to Congress, Lantos had little in the way of Boeing shares. But he kept buying and buying, year after year. According to his last financial disclosures, Lantos ended up owning between $1 million and $5 million of stock in the airplane maker. This when his total net worth was between $1.9 and $11 million.[24]

Lantos did very well with his investment. When he first arrived in Congress, Boeing stock was trading at $5 a share. By the time he died in 2008, it was $85 a share. It's hard not to come to the conclusion that Lantos had something to do with Boeing's success.

So why did Lantos tie up so much of his wealth in the fortunes of one company? It probably had something to do with the fact that because of his congressional position, he had an extraordinary amount of influence over the health of Boeing. Lantos served as chairman and ranking member of the House Committee on Foreign Affairs, which had direct oversight of the Export-Import Bank, a little-known federal agency that operates as one of the most blatant examples of corporate welfare in America. (Both the libertarian Cato Institute and Senator Bernie Sanders, a self-professed socialist, have denounced the Export-Import Bank as "corporate welfare at its worst.") Created at the height of the Great

Depression, the bank had the goal of boosting American manufacturing.

Today, the Ex-Im Bank is often referred to as "Boeing's bank." The bank helped fund more than 25% of the airliners Boeing delivered in 2009, for example. In 2008, the year Lantos died, Boeing deals accounted for almost 40% of the bank's $21 billion in business. Boeing is a major manufacturer in the United States, to be sure, but the amount of support it receives is totally out of proportion to its size. The recent Ex-Im investments are actually down from their height. In 1999, 75% of the Export-Import Bank's financing went to Boeing. That same year, shareholders like Lantos saw the stock price jump from $32 to $45 a share.[25]

About 2% of all U.S. exports get Ex-Im financing; about 20% of Boeing's business does. In other words, it's ten times more likely to get funds than are other exporters.[26] As the *Wall Street Journal* put it, "No company has deeper relations with Ex-Im Bank than Chicago-based Boeing."[27]

Lantos was a champion of Ex-Im, fighting off efforts by conservative Republicans to end it and aggressively pushing for its reauthorization. He was a tireless advocate of a government program that was directly benefiting his largest single stock asset.

Honest graft is so insidious because it piggybacks on legitimate service, and cloaks both in the name of public good.

Give someone the chance to feel that they are serving the public and getting rich at the same time and you have created a nightmare. Always a practical observer of human nature, Benjamin Franklin in 1787 expressed concern to the Constitutional Convention that when you give politicians the opportunity to "do good and do well" you are asking for trouble: "There are two passions which have a powerful influence in the affairs of men. These are *ambition* and *avarice*; the love of power and the love of money. Separately, each of these has great force in prompting men to action; but when united in view of the same object, they have in many minds the most violent effects. Place before the eyes of such men a post of *honor* that shall at the same time be a place of *profit*, and they will move heaven and earth to obtain it."

Ben Franklin knew human nature. He would not have been surprised by the deep sense of entitlement claimed by the Government Rich. Because of their "public service" and "sacrifice" to us, they feel entitled to the manipulation of the business market for their own benefit. Their attitude is that the rules that apply to the rest of us—insider trading laws, conflict-of-interest statutes—don't apply to them *and never should*. The Permanent Political Class is, and expects to continue to be, untouchable.

The Permanent Political Class does not produce any goods or services. Their ability to make money rises from their ability to extract wealth by leveraging it from others. Politicians can write legislation that can destroy corporations or help them prosper. They can perform constituent services to benefit friends or punish enemies. They can intervene with bureaucrats in a way that can reap billions for a company. They have access to information that can dramatically affect the economy and financial markets, information that few other people have.

All of this crony capitalism comes at a high price for the rest of us. Under free market capitalism, the idea is that a rising tide lifts all boats. Henry Ford wanted Americans to become more prosperous because then he could sell them more cars. Crony capitalism is a zero-sum game. Crony capitalists don't care whether a rising tide lifts all boats. They just want to buy their way onto the big party boat.

All too often people assume that corporations and special interests have the real power and that politicians are mere corks tossed around in the rough surf of capitalism. The fact is that the Permanent Political Class has immense formal and informal powers that are both blunt and subtle. For example, your chance of getting audited by the Internal Revenue Service often depends on who your congressman is. One study found that the IRS actually shifts enforcement away from congressional districts represented by legislators who sit on committees with oversight of the IRS.[28]

A study by Stanford University's Rock Center for Corporate Governance found evidence that firms that make political contributions and hire lobbyists are less likely to face enforcement actions by the Securities and Exchange Commission. And if they are subject to an SEC enforcement action, they are likely "to face lower penalties on average."[29]

Two professors found that companies that hire lobbyists are, on average, much less likely to be detected for fraud, or they can evade detection for 117 days longer than average. These firms are also 38% less likely to be detected by regulators. The scholars note that "the delay in detection leads to a greater distortion in resource allocation during fraudulent periods. It also allows managers to sell more of their shares." Having friends in Washington can be extremely valuable.[30]

Washington's financial leveraging power can be found even in something as seemingly innocuous as the Endangered Species Act (ESA). The act can have an enormous economic effect on property owners and developers. Scholars at Auburn University found that the implementation of the ESA has been highly political. Politics determine which species gets listed as threatened or endangered and how quickly (or slowly) a certain species gets recognized and protected. The researchers found that states with House members on the budget oversight subcommittee responsible for funding the U.S. Fish and Wildlife Service and the Environmental Protection Agency had significantly fewer listings than other states. As the researchers put it, "Congressional representatives who sit on the Interior subcommittee of the House Appropriations Committee use their position to shield their constituents, at least partially, from the adverse consequences of ESA."[31]

By looking at Department of Housing and Urban Development grants designed to combat economic blight and help "distressed" cities, researchers found that there was no evidence that these factors had any real effect on how the HUD grants were awarded. The decisions were instead based on political influence, by bureaucrats rewarding friends.[32]

Has anything really changed since George Washington Plunkitt's day? The methods, techniques, and tools are similar. But while Tammany Hall corruption controlled a city, today's crony capitalism is about a system that operates at the highest levels of an entire nation.

There is a lot of money sloshing around in the nation's capital. As of 2010, seven of the ten richest counties in the United States were in the Washington, D.C., area. During the Great Recession of 2008–2009, Washington boasted the best-performing real estate market in the country. What is it that drives the D.C. economy? Not private enterprise, certainly. And we can only expect these trends to continue, unless we make changes.[33]

The upper tiers of the U.S. economy are increasingly a network of individuals who make special deals with politicians—and the politicians themselves. The distinction between the public and private sectors has become blurred. More than half of the Fortune 1000 companies have an ex-politician or ex-bureaucrat sitting on their corporate boards.

Before plunging into the specifics and key offenders of modern crony capitalism, we need to ask: How is this possible, and why does our system of laws allow all this to happen? As you will see, the answer isn't simply a matter of overlooked corruption. The system of crony capitalism has powerful defenders.

The bank robber Willie Sutton was once asked why he robbed banks. His well-known response: "Because that's where the money is." Why has crony capitalism become so widespread? The response is the same. Let's take a look at how the crony insiders get their loot.

Part One

CONGRESSIONAL CRONIES

1

THE DRUG TRADE

OVER THE PAST half century there has been a massive web woven between the federal government and the health care industry. Whether due to special taxes, fines, regulations, subsidies, or mandates, there have been enormous sums of money at stake in governmental decision-making for health care companies—and the companies' investors. By 2007, federal government programs like Medicare, Medicaid, and others accounted for 46% of all health care spending in the United States.[1] Knowing what changes might be in store for those programs, and having advance notice of details of other health care legislation, could translate into a lot of profits. For a sitting United States senator, trading stocks at the same time you are pushing and writing legislation could net you millions in capital gains.

Throughout 2009, Washington was consumed by the Patient Protection and Affordable Care Act, or what became commonly known (at least to its critics) as Obamacare. It began as a campaign promise, became a debate, and ended with horse-trading, political threats, and partisan muscle. The bill that was eventually passed by Congress and signed by President Obama was 2,500 pages long. Very few members actually knew everything that was in the bill or what it all meant. Some members had not even had a chance to read it. The health care industry and pharmaceutical companies employed thousands of lobbyists to shape the legislation. When the dust finally settled, clear winners and losers emerged. The details that determined who came out ahead and who didn't were almost always hammered out behind closed doors. A single event could cause the price of a stock to swing wildly. For example, when six senators announced on July 27, 2009, that they were going to eliminate the "public option"—a government-run insurance policy—from their version of the health care reform bill, the share prices of three major insurance companies surged by between 8% and 10% the next day. Trading stocks in such an environment could be highly profitable, especially if you knew about such events in advance.

One of those at the center of shaping the bill was Senator John Kerry of Massachusetts. Kerry, first elected to the Senate in 1984, had been a longtime advocate of health care reform. He serves as a member of the Health Subcommittee on the powerful Senate Finance Committee. The former Democratic nominee for President is a member of the wealthy Forbes family and is the beneficiary of at least four inherited trusts. In 1995, his wealth jumped dramatically when he married Teresa Heinz, the widow of Pennsylvania Senator John Heinz, heir to the Heinz family fortune. Teresa Heinz Kerry is worth hundreds of millions of dollars.

Like other very wealthy people, John Kerry is an investor. His family trusts are relatively small, worth less than $1 million, according to his 2009 financial disclosures. By themselves they could hardly sustain his lifestyle. The bulk of the Kerrys' wealth resides in a series of marital trust and commingled fund accounts. All together, these funds include significant investments in stocks of many corporations. It is his buying and selling of health care stocks during the debate over health care reform that is particularly interesting. While some have reported that the Kerrys' assets are in a blind trust, they have not been designated as such on his financial disclosure forms.[2]

Contrary to public perception, the major pharmaceutical companies were in favor of Obama's health care bill. The President's new program was expected to increase the demand for prescription drugs by making health care more accessible. Big Pharma, as the companies are collectively known, decided it could not stop the bill, so it might as well try to influence its provisions. Back in 1994, when the Clinton administration (and notably Hillary Clinton) had pushed for dramatic changes in the health care system, several effective ads sponsored by the pharmaceutical industry, starring "Harry and Louise," helped defeat "Hillarycare." In 2009, Big Pharma hired the two actors again. Only this time they were fifteen years older—and they were in favor of the bill. "Well, it looks like we may finally get health care reform," said Harry, in one ad.

In July 2009, industry representatives met with key members of Congress and hashed out critical details of the new Obama bill.[3] As the bill snaked its way through the House and Senate, where Kerry was actively pushing it, the Kerrys began buying stock in the drug maker Teva Pharmaceuticals as the prospects of its passage improved. In November alone they bought close to $750,000 in the company.[4]

When the Kerrys first began buying shares, the stock was trading at around $50. After health care reform passed, it surged to

$62. In 2010, after the reform bill was signed, the Kerrys sold some of their shares in Teva, reaping tens of thousands in capital gains. (It's unclear exactly how much because of the way the transactions are reported. Politicians are required to report ranges only—not exact dollar amounts.) And they held on to more than $1 million worth of Teva shares. All in all, health care stocks proved to be some of the Kerrys' best investments that year, in terms of return on investment.

To be sure, Senator Kerry wasn't the only congressional trader in pharmaceuticals. John Tanner of Tennessee, a member of the House Ways and Means Committee, bought up to $90,000 worth back in April 2009, when the House was approving reserve-fund budgeting for health care (part of the annual budget process). Also buying Teva were Senator Jim Webb of Virginia and Congressman Vern Buchanan of Florida. Unlike Kerry and Webb, however, Buchanan voted against the bill. Casting a vote is one thing; betting on the final tally is something else. Most members, most of the time, know full well which bills will pass before they cast their votes. Health care was such an important bill, and the Democrats had such a strong majority (even if Scott Brown's surprise election in Massachusetts denied them a supermajority of sixty votes in the Senate), that opposing members like Vern Buchanan could still place bets that the bill would eventually get to Obama's desk.

The very idea that politicians trade stocks while they are considering major bills comes as a shock to many people, but it is standard behavior in Washington. Senator Tom Carper of Delaware sat next to Kerry on the Senate Finance Committee's Health Subcommittee. Carper, more of a centrist than Kerry, was concerned about the public option. And according to former Senator Tom Daschle, who was a point man in the Obama administration's push to pass the bill, Carper was intimately involved in hammering together the health care bill throughout the spring

PRIMING THE PUMP

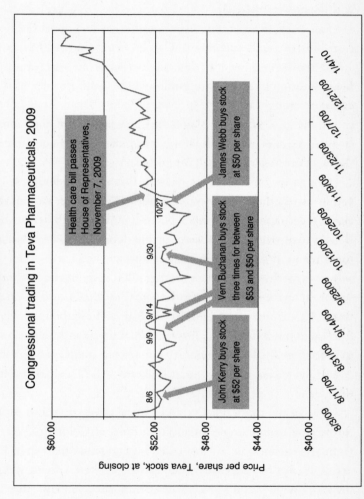

Congressional trading in Teva Pharmaceuticals, 2009

and summer of 2009. By the fall he'd joined a group known as the Gang of Ten, who were trying to bring about a compromise with Republicans.[5]

Just a few weeks after three committees had approved health care bills in rapid succession, Carper began buying health care stocks that would benefit from the legislation he was supporting. He bought up to $50,000 in Nationwide Health Properties, a real estate investment trust that specialized in health care–related properties. He also picked up shares in Cardinal Health and CareFusion. (As we will see, Cardinal was a popular investment choice for those involved in the health care debate.)

Congresswoman Melissa Bean of Illinois, a moderate, seemed torn over whether to vote for or against Obamacare. But her indecision didn't apply to her stock portfolio. Along with her husband, Bean traded shares as she watched the debate unfold in Washington. Indeed, although Bean and her husband are active traders, the *only stock purchases* they made during 2009 were in the health care sector. They bought shares in Cardinal Health, CareFusion, and two drug manufacturers, Mylan and Teva. Bean bought Teva in April at about $46 a share. After Obamacare passed, shares soared to more than $63. She bought Mylan when it traded at $14 a share. After Obamacare became law, it rocketed to $23 a share, up more than 50%.[6]

One of the more creative and cynical plays on health care reform came from Congressman Jared Polis of Colorado. Polis is a young politician who had just taken his congressional seat in January 2009. But he was clearly seen as a rising star, with an appointment to the powerful House Rules Committee. He also sits on the House Democratic Steering and Policy Committee and on the Education and Labor Committee's Subcommittee on Healthy Families and Communities. Polis is wealthy. He grew up amid privilege, and his family became enormously rich after founding and later selling Bluemountain.com, the greeting card website.

Throughout 2009, Polis was a tireless advocate for Obamacare, declaring that health care reform "could not come at a better time." Polis sat on two House committees that were central to the crafting and passage of the health care bill. As a member of the House Education and Labor Committee, he was involved in shepherding through one of the three pieces of legislation that would become the final bill. And as a member of the powerful Rules Committee, he helped shape the parameters and procedures to secure passage of the bill in the House.

None of this gave him pause when it came to investing in health care companies as he helped determine the fate of Obamacare. While Polis was praising the benefits of health care overhaul, he was buying millions of dollars' worth of a private company called BridgeHealth International.[7] BridgeHealth describes itself as a "leading health care strategic consultancy." It works with companies to help them cut health care costs. One of the things that BridgeHealth offers is medical tourism: providing less expensive medical procedures in countries such as China, Mexico, India, Thailand, Costa Rica, and Taiwan. In other words, Polis was betting that there would be more, not less, medical tourism after the passage of health care reform. Companies in the medical tourism industry generally agreed, and favored Obamacare. They did not believe the bill would actually contain costs, and if anything, they expected overseas medical procedures to become more attractive. *Medical Tourism* magazine featured an article after the passage of the bill entitled, "Medical Tourism Expands as Alternative to Obamacare." As the article put it, "Interest in medical tourism has expanded rapidly as Americans react to the new federal law."[8]

After the reform bill became law, BridgeHealth boasted that

it was uniquely positioned to help companies cut medical costs. "What we can offer to the employer and insurer is health care reform today because we've addressed quality and cost," Vic Lazzaro, BridgeHealth's CEO, said in July 2010 after the bill was passed. "This is an opportunity to convert that Cadillac plan to a Buick because you can reduce that cost."[9]

In all, Polis put between $7 million and $35 million into the company as the health care bill wended its way through Capitol Hill. When investment timing was crucial, Polis's purchases often coincided with the work of his committees. As the Education and Labor Committee considered health care reform in June and July, he made two large purchases of company stock, worth between $1 million and $5 million, on June 16 and 17. His committee passed the health care bill in mid-July. By October 2009, it was Polis's powerful Rules Committee that was determining which amendments would be considered and what the parameters of the debate would be as the House worked to pass the same legislation that was moving forward in the Senate. On October 13 and 23, Polis made two more purchases of shares worth between $1 million and $5 million. Polis's office, not surprisingly, insists that his investments had no influence on his vote. (It was all a coincidence!) But people do not make multimillion-dollar investments in a vacuum. And Polis was well positioned to know the details of the massive bill as well as what amendments would or wouldn't be considered.

Then there is the matter of his biotech investments. The health care reform bill that emerged from Polis's committees was also enormously beneficial for biotech companies. Embedded in the complex bill were two clauses that were vital for the profitability of these companies. The first was the Therapeutic Discovery Project Credit, which provided a 50% credit for investments in biotech pharmaceutical research. Far more important was the Approval Pathway for Biosimilar Biological Products. The Food and Drug Administration gives traditional branded prescription drugs five years of exclusivity before a generic version of the same medication can be produced. But in this provision, biotech drugs were given a twelve-year exclusivity.

Many observers, like Dr. Jerry Avorn and Dr. Aaron Kesselheim of Harvard University, believed that the twelve-year period was unjustified and that five years was plenty of time. That was the position of the FDA itself.[10] The longer window would, of course, be a boon to biotech investors. As biotech analyst Richard Gayle put it after the law passed, "Biotechnology companies now have a known period of market exclusivity post-approval, one that is independent of patent time frames. This will provide investors with the predictability they crave when they project product sales far into the future for biotech drugs in development." In the health care bill, he said, the biotech industry "got exactly what it wanted."[11]

Congressman Polis favored the discovery credit and longer-exclusivity provisions. And he made three large purchases of an exchange-traded fund when his committees pushed through the bill. He bought between $750,000 and $1.5 million in the PowerShares Dynamic Biotech and Genome ETF just weeks after the committee proposed to extend the exclusivity period. He bought the fund at about $16 per share. After Obamacare passed, the price jumped to $20, a 25% increase in six months.

How much money did Polis make? We will probably never know. Curiously, having made these aggressive transactions throughout 2009, in January 2010 he suddenly converted his assets to a "qualified blind trust." As we will see later, these blind trusts are not really blind, and they don't prevent a politician from providing political intelligence to those who manage the accounts. In Polis's case, the person handling his trust was a longtime friend and large campaign contributor named Solomon Halpern. By creating the blind trust, Polis no longer had to disclose his stock transactions or profits.

Meanwhile, John and Teresa Heinz Kerry continued to trade. Along with Teva, during 2009 the Kerrys also picked up shares in ResMed—at least $200,000 worth. ResMed makes medical devices such as airway aids for sufferers of sleep apnea. The Kerrys managed to snatch up shares in the $20-to-$25 range. After health care reform passed, shares in the company surged to $34, as much as 71% higher than what the Kerrys paid for them. (Two years later, in the spring of 2011, ResMed's stock price had fallen back below $30.) ResMed was a winner in the health care reform legislation—as Reuters declared—thanks in part to John Kerry's efforts. In early versions of the health care bill, device makers like ResMed were to be taxed, starting in 2010, through an "industry fee." In the final bill, fees for medical device makers were delayed until 2013, and the industry tax was replaced by a smaller sales tax (2.3%). Kerry was a strong opponent of higher taxes on medical device makers.

The Kerrys also bought between $250,000 and $500,000 in Thermo Fisher Scientific, which provides products and services to hospitals and medical centers. The firm had a lot at stake with health care reform. The Kerrys bought the stake at around $35 a share. After the reform bill became law, the stock was selling at more than $50 a share—a jump of more than 40%.

While the Kerrys were buying Obamacare winners, they were dumping losers. In the final bill, pharma was a winner, the health insurance industry was a big loser. Not coincidentally, the Kerrys had been selling all their stock in health insurance companies. One such company, United Health, offers Medicare insurance. The legislation dictated lower reimbursements for Medicare procedures.

Lifetime coverage limits and protection against preexisting medical conditions were removed—extremely popular aspects of the bill, to be sure, but they squeezed United Health's bottom line. By the end of June 2009, the Kerrys had sold all of their shares in United Health. They also dropped their investment in Wellpoint, another health benefits company. Six weeks later, Kerry introduced an amendment to tax generous health care plans, which would clearly hurt companies like those whose stock he had just sold.[12]

Kerry's profitable history of congressional trading does not begin and end with the debate over President Obama's bill in 2009. Indeed, some of his most dramatic and amazingly well-timed trades occurred earlier, during other health-care-related high-stakes legislative battles. Some of his biggest scores were tied to his knowledge of obscure matters that had huge ramifications for certain companies.

In May 2007, a government agency called the Federal Center for Medicare and Medicaid Services was looking at two drugs that were used to treat anemia in cancer patients. The agency had to decide: Did Johnson & Johnson's Procrit and Amgen's Aranesp warrant reimbursement under Medicare? Johnson & Johnson was a large, diversified company with lots of products, so rejection of its drug would not be critical. But for Amgen, losing Medicare reimbursement for Aranesp would be a disaster. The drug was commonly given to elderly cancer patients, many of whom could afford it only under Medicare.

Indeed, when the word went out that the government might end the reimbursements, Amgen shares plunged. But at least one investor avoided those losses with two nearly perfectly timed trades. On May 4, the Kerrys sold between $250,000 and $500,000 in Amgen stock. Three days later, they sold the balance of their stock in the company, another $250,000 to $500,000, when it closed at $63.76

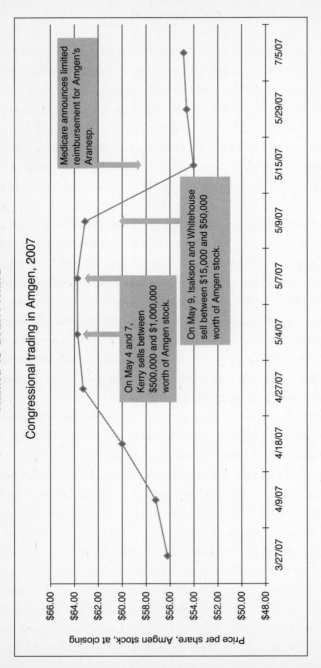

TIMING IS EVERYTHING

Congressional trading in Amgen, 2007

Medicare announces limited reimbursement for Amgen's Aranesp.

On May 4 and 7, Kerry sells between $500,000 and $1,000,000 worth of Amgen stock.

On May 9, Isakson and Whitehouse sell between $15,000 and $50,000 worth of Amgen stock.

Price per share, Amgen stock, at closing

$66.00
$64.00
$62.00
$60.00
$58.00
$56.00
$54.00
$52.00
$50.00
$48.00

3/27/07 4/9/07 4/18/07 4/27/07 5/4/07 5/7/07 5/9/07 5/15/07 5/29/07 7/5/07

per share. If they had waited two weeks, these sales would have been worth between $50,000 and $100,000 less, because on May 15 it was publicly announced that Medicare would sharply limit reimbursements for treatment with Aranesp. The price dropped to $54.01, or down 15%.[13]

Joining Senator Kerry in dumping Amgen shares just in time were two senators who sat on the Health, Education, Labor, and Pensions Committee, which did not have direct oversight of Medicare but was involved in health and pharmaceutical policies in general. Senators Johnny Isakson and Sheldon Whitehouse both sold between $15,000 and $50,000 worth of Amgen stock on the same day, May 9, also avoiding large losses.[14] Did Senator Kerry know the news was coming? Did Senators Isakson and Whitehouse know anything? We cannot be sure. If they had worked in the private sector, their access and timing would almost certainly have demanded an SEC investigation. Short of sworn testimony, we cannot rule out that they simply guessed right, or were lucky. Even in the private sector, they might not be proven guilty. But the timing seems far too good to be true.

A few years before this narrow pharmaceutical debate, the Kerrys went on a big stock-buying spree involving more than one hundred health care transactions over a period of several months. The end result was capital gains of at least $500,000, and possibly as high as $2 million. It happened in 2003, when Congress was debating what would become the largest overhaul of the Medicare program in its thirty-eight-year history. The Medicare Prescription Drug, Improvement, and Modernization Act created a new entitlement benefit for prescription drugs. The drug manufacturers were all for it, and why wouldn't they be? Under the bill's provisions the federal government would pay part of the cost of prescription drugs for all 44.8 million elderly and disabled beneficiaries. Health insurance companies were for it too, because the money would flow through them.

The new benefit, called Medicare Part D, subsidized approximately the first $2,500 of a senior citizen's prescription drug costs. En route to final passage, two versions of the bill emerged. One cleared the House on June 27, 2003, and the other passed the Senate on July 7. One called for a cap on drug prices, the other did not. The drug industry stood to gain more with one than the other, but either way, the gain would be huge. Congress went into a joint conference committee on November 21 to iron out differences. It was finally signed by President George W. Bush on December 8, with no caps on drug prices.

Throughout the process, senators and representatives were buying and selling pharmaceutical stocks that would be hurt by or benefit from the legislation. Yet not everyone succumbed to temptation. Perhaps no congressman held more stock in branded pharmaceutical companies than James Sensenbrenner of Wisconsin, who owned between $1 million and $5 million in Merck stock, $500,000 in Abbott Labs, and between $700,000 and $1.2 million in Pfizer stock. To his credit, Sensenbrenner didn't trade stock during the debate.[15]

By contrast, Congressman James Oberstar of Minnesota quietly sold off his shares in the generic drug manufacturer Pharmaceutical Resources (now Par Pharmaceuticals) on September 22 and October 17 as the bill moved toward passage. He sold his holdings when the stock was selling at more than $70 a share. After Bush signed the bill, shares plummeted to $40 within a few months, as generic drug makers lost some competitive advantage to name-brand drug providers. Three days before President Bush signed the Medicare legislation into law, Oberstar also sold his shares in HealthExtras (now Catalyst Health Solutions), a pharmacy insurance management services firm. After Bush signed, the stock lost close to 10% of its value.[16]

Oberstar had been in Congress since 1975 and knew the ways of Washington. Congressman Jeb Bradley of New Hampshire had just been seated in January 2003, yet he apparently was a quick learner. Bradley owned over $300,000 in pharmaceutical stock when he took office. By October, he'd bought additional shares of Pfizer, Merck, and Johnson & Johnson before voting in favor of the prescription drug benefit.[17] Merck stock jumped 10% in the weeks following President Bush's signing of the law. Pfizer and Johnson & Johnson were both up too.

By far the most aggressive congressional trading of pharma stock during this debate was done by Senator John Kerry and his wife. Oversight of the prescription drug plan would fall to Kerry's committee in the Senate, so he was intimately familiar with the law and its ramifications. Kerry was opposed to key portions of the legislation and wanted to allow for the importation of drugs from Canada to keep drug prices down. But when it became apparent that importation of drugs would not pass, the Kerrys became increasingly aggressive in buying up pharma stock. In all, the Kerrys made a stunning 111 transactions of pharmaceutical companies and health insurance companies in 2003, according to his financial disclosure statements.[18] They were all great picks. He bought shares of drug makers as well as the health plan companies that would actually administer the plan through Medicare. For example, throughout September Kerry made nine purchases of Johnson & Johnson stock, totaling more than $500,000.[19]

The Kerrys also made sixteen purchases of Pfizer stock, totaling as much as $1 million, while the legislation was being worked on in committee. When he bought the stock it was hovering in the $30 range. After the Medicare drug benefit bill passed, the stock rose to $36 a share—up 20%. On November 13 and 17, 2003, he bought at least $200,000 worth of stock in Oxford Health Plans, which provides coverage for prescription drugs. He also bought between $500,000 and $1 million of stock in United Health Group, which happened to become the largest health insurance provider under Medicare Plan D after the legislation passed. Kerry's financial disclosure statements reveal that the amount he had invested United Health by the end of the year was between $1 million and $5 million. He bought the stock in November at around $28 a share. Months later, it was trading at $33. There were also four purchases of stock in Abbott Labs in the month of November, when it was trading at $44 a share. After Medicare Plan D passed, share prices moved up to $46. The Kerrys also bought Bristol-Myers Squibb, which was trading at around $26 a share. The stock rocketed to more than $39 after the prescription drug benefit became law.

The Kerrys also purchased shares of Cardinal Health, another Medicare Plan D provider (at least $100,000 worth), and made four purchases of Merck stock in November, of at least $240,000.[20]

In addition to helping drug manufacturers, the Medicare Prescription Drug Act also provided for add-on payments for certain new medical devices. The Kerrys were already invested in two venture funds focused on medical technologies, Salix Ventures II and Delphi. In 2003, they upped their investments in both. The following year they reaped capital gains of between $100,000 and $1 million.

In January 2004, after President Bush signed the law and the stock prices jumped, the Kerrys started selling some of their pharma stocks. The couple netted capital gains of between $100,000 and $1 million with their Oxford Health Plans investment alone. They also netted tens of thousands of dollars in capital gains from Pfizer, Johnson & Johnson, and Cardinal Health stocks.

It was an enormously aggressive short-term bet on pharma stock. If you look at the Kerrys' trades in other sectors throughout 2003 — transportation, blue chips, and high tech, among others — you find a regular mix of buys and sells. But of the 111 transactions involving health plans and pharma stock, 103 were buys.[21]

The health care debate in 2009 was a much bigger event than any of these predecessors. As we have seen, John Kerry was not alone in buying and selling shares as Congress worked to remake the health care system. Some of the most powerful men in the Senate were part of the action. At the center of forging the health care bill was Senator Max Baucus of Montana. Eventually, when the major health care and pharmaceutical companies came out in favor of the bill, it was partly thanks to a series of detailed set-asides that were of immense benefit to the industry. Baucus had a lot of influence on those set-asides because he had been tasked by the White House and by congressional Democrats to put the deal together. And during the legislative process, Senator Baucus, as he was negotiating with pharmaceutical companies and putting his imprint on the legislation, was buying and selling health care stocks. Baucus does not do a lot of stock trading, and he's not a wealthy man. He is no John Kerry. Indeed, he's not even in Kerry's financial universe. But during 2009, as he was shepherding health care legislation in the Senate, fully 20% of Baucus's stock transactions involved health care–related stocks. He bought Gilead Sciences, Abbott Labs, and Fluor Corporation (which is not a health care company but is heavily involved in the sector, building hospitals and medical care centers). All three were perceived winners in the health care debate. And he seemed to do pretty well. He bought Abbott at around $45 a share. After health care reform passed, it soared to $54 a share. All three firms lobbied in favor of the legislation.[22]

Congressman John Boehner, who was leading the opposition to Obamacare in the House of Representatives, may have been fighting John Kerry on policy matters, but he was entirely allied with him when it came to investment decisions. On December 10, 2009, Boehner bought numerous health insurance company stocks, including tens of thousands of dollars in Cardinal Health, Cigna, and Wellpoint. On the same day, Boehner purchased shares in the Big Pharma companies Amgen, Johnson & Johnson, Forest Labs, Covidien, and Pfizer. He also bought shares in CareFusion, which provides systems for countering infections.[23] Just days later, on December 15, the *Washington Post* declared that the "public option" was officially dead.[24]

Health insurers breathed a sigh of relief. So too did pharmaceutical companies, who feared that a government health insurance program would lead to price controls. When Boehner bought Wellpoint stock on December 10, the price was about $56 a share. Within a month it was trading at $66 a share. Cardinal Health was up approximately 10% by the time President Obama signed the health care bill. In early 2010, Boehner bought yet more shares in Cardinal Health and Pfizer, before President Obama signed the health care bill.

Sometimes members of Congress see an opportunity for big profits from a smaller, more obscure bill (health-related or otherwise). This approach has certain advantages. The chances of being detected are smaller, and if the focus of the bill is narrow enough, it can mean even more profits. Such was the case in the spring and early summer of 2004, as Congress debated and eventually passed something called Project Bioshield.

Concerned about the possibility of a biological weapons attack or the prospect of a pandemic, legislators submitted a bill that called for $5 billion to be spent on vaccines that would be used in

the event of a bioterrorist attack or disease outbreak. The idea behind Project Bioshield was simple: pour billions into small, special-
ized biotech companies that were developing vaccines and other
biochemical defenses. The Department of Health and Human
Services was moving forward with plans to acquire a second-gen-
eration smallpox vaccine and antidotes to other chemical, biological, and radiological weapons. The government wanted to develop,
purchase, and stockpile vaccines and drugs to fight anthrax, smallpox, and other potential agents of bioterror.

The largest financial beneficiaries of this money would be spe-
cialized biotechnology companies. The bill sailed through both
houses of Congress and was signed by President Bush on July 21,
2004. But in the weeks before Bush acted, several congressmen
made highly profitable "bets" on the companies that would benefit.

Congressman Jim McDermott of Washington State bet big on
one small biotech company as Project Bioshield was working its
way through the House. McDermott, a member of the powerful
Ways and Means Committee and a medical doctor by training,
took more than 10% of his entire investment portfolio at Wells
Fargo and bought shares in a small Canadian company called ID
Biomedical on June 7, 2004, just weeks before he voted for the
bill. The firm just happened to produce disease vaccines, exactly
the kind that Project Bioshield was looking to fund. Over the next
several years, the firm would do a considerable amount of business with the federal government. With the passage of Project
Bioshield, ID Biomedical would secure $8 million from Washing-
ton to develop a plague vaccine.[25] McDermott's timing was nearly
perfect. He bought 2,000 shares at $10 a share, paying a total of
$21,021, according to his brokerage statement. He sold the stock
a little more than a year later, on September 21, 2005, nearly tri-
pling his money, cashing it in for $58,837. This represents a return
of 180%.[26]

McDermott was not alone. Congressman Amo Houghton, Republican of New York, saw his investment portfolio mushroom with biodefense medical stocks in the weeks before Project Bioshield became law. His investment fund bought about $30,000 in Avant Immunotherapeutics (now called Celldex) on July 15, 16, 19, and 21, just days before President Bush signed the bill. The company was developing next-generation anthrax-fighting drugs and would do significant business through Project Bioshield. Houghton also gobbled up shares in Nanogen, a biomedical company, twice, on July 12 and 15. And he bought $17,355 in Northfield Labs on July 14 and another $16,792 the next day. Northfield was developing blood-replacement alternatives and would get grants from the U.S. Army through Bioshield. On July 15, Houghton bought almost $20,000 of Hollis-Eden Pharmaceuticals, which was developing disease management technologies. On the same day, he bought almost $35,000 in Maxim Pharmaceuticals, which produces antiviral drugs. The next day, July 16, he went back for more shares of Hollis-Eden, bringing his total holdings to almost $40,000.[27] All of these companies would benefit from the infusion of federal dollars. If it's possible to overdose on drugs and make money from it, that is what Houghton managed to do.[28]

Before he served in Congress, Houghton had a long career in corporate America as CEO of Corning and as a member of several corporate boards. If, as a corporate CEO, he had executed these trades based on insider information—concerning, say, a merger—it might have been problematic. It certainly would have received the attention of the SEC. But as a member of Congress, this sort of behavior is acceptable and commonplace.

We despise professional athletes who bet on their own games. Why don't we feel the same way about politicians who bet on the outcome of legislation? The stakes are surely higher.

2

CRISIS FOR ALL,
OPPORTUNITY FOR SOME

IN THE SUMMER and fall of 2008, the world economy hovered on the brink of catastrophe. A combination of too much bad debt and a burst housing market bubble threatened to push the American economy over the edge, with much of the rest of the world likely to follow. In Washington, D.C., dramatic and historic decisions involving trillions of dollars were made in rapid succession in an effort to contain the crisis. The Permanent Political Class played a central role in the drama as the government broke precedent after precedent.

For members of Congress, the crisis meant momentous votes, long hours in closed-door meetings, and countless phone calls with federal officials. It also meant regular private consultations on both budgetary and monetary decisions. It meant private conversations with Wall Street and banking executives. It meant emergency measures, including authorizing the spending of $700 billion in taxpayer money in an attempt to create liquidity in financial markets—the Troubled Asset Relief Program, a.k.a. TARP.

And for certain members of Congress, it also meant trading stocks at critical times.

One of those who played a central role in governmental decisionmaking during the crisis was Congressman Spencer Bachus, then the ranking Republican on the House Financial Services Committee. (When Republicans retook control of the House of Representatives in 2010, Bachus became chairman.) It was the Financial Services Committee through which all bailout and other financial legislation had to move. When President George W. Bush discussed the passage of the Emergency Economic Stabilization Act in the midst of the crisis, he praised six members of Congress for their work on the issue, Bachus among them.[1] But beyond the formal hearings on the legislation, Bachus was regularly involved in private meetings and phone conversations. As he recounted later, he "received repeated Saturday or Sunday calls announcing intervention after intervention" by the government in the financial markets.[2] Henry Paulson, who was the Treasury secretary at the time, recounts in his memoir numerous closed-door meetings at which Bachus was a participant.[3]

As he was having those high-level discussions, however, he was also aggressively buying and selling stock options. For his efforts, Bachus netted tens of thousands of dollars in capital gains, while most Americans watched their portfolios plummet. A lawyer and a former state senator, Bachus has served in Congress since 1993. He is not a wealthy man. According to his financial disclosure forms, his net worth is less than $1 million. But he is an active stock trader. He is particularly active when it comes to trading options, which is a relatively inexpensive way to bet that a particular stock, or the broader market, will go up or down.

If you think a stock will fall from its current price, you can buy an option to sell it at that current price, without spending the money to own the stock itself. If the price drops from, say, $4 to $2, you can buy it at $2 and immediately exercise your right to sell it at $4. If you bet wrong, you can let your option expire without ever buying the stock. Bachus has used this investment strategy repeatedly to supplement his salary. One year, for example, he earned as much from his options trading as he did from his congressional salary. Here's the rub: all too often his trades coincided with his congressional work.

From July 2008, when the first murmurs of the crisis were heard, to the dark days of November, with international markets in near free fall, Bachus engineered no less than forty options trades, betting that the market, a sector of the market, or an individual company would go up or down at critical times.

Financial markets were experiencing the greatest volatility on record.[4] Trillions of dollars in stock profits were being washed away. But for Bachus it was different. According to his financial disclosure statements, Bachus netted as much as $50,000 in capital gains by aggressively playing the market during this volatile period. And he netted tens of thousands more in early 2009, when financial reforms were put in place. What makes these results impressive is the fact that options trading is extremely risky. There is a rule of thumb in the financial industry that 75% of options are worthless when it comes time to redeem them, and that 80% of options traders lose money.

In a speech he gave shortly after the financial crisis abated, Bachus noted that the political class was looking at policy and making decisions on "how the markets were reacting."[5] Unfortunately, Bachus was also trading on that same information.

In the summer heat of 2008, as the crisis was getting started and before a broader panic set in, there were concerns about the housing market and the health of banks in particular. It was not fully apparent that the entire financial system might be at risk. Some banks had failed, the investment house of Lehman Brothers had been battered but had not yet failed (it would finally go under on September 15), and government-backed Fannie Mae and Freddie Mac were in serious financial trouble. Bachus's Financial Services Committee consulted regularly with federal officials and was considering a series of legislative steps to deal with these problems.

Fannie Mae (the Federal National Mortgage Association) and Freddie Mac (the Federal Home Loan Mortgage Corporation) are congressionally chartered corporations whose original purpose was to pump cash into the nation's mortgage market. By 2007, the two had $83.2 billion in assets—but they were also carrying about $5.2 trillion in debt and guarantees. In short, they were leveraged at a ratio of about 65 to 1, and were hardly sustainable as the housing market tumbled.[6] Both were deeply in trouble and effectively insolvent. If they went down, many feared that Fannie and Freddie might bring the entire financial system down with them, since it would mean widespread foreclosures on countless homes. To head off disaster, congressional leaders and administration officials conferred frequently. According to Henry Paulson's memoir, for example, a private meeting took place on September 4 in the Russell Senate Office Building, with Paulson, Senators Chris Dodd and Richard Shelby, and Congressman Bachus in attendance. During the meeting they discussed how to proceed with legislation to rescue Fannie and Freddie. There had also been congressional hearings and consultations in July and August.[7]

As Bachus and his committee wrestled with these issues, the congressman was aggressively buying options.[8] Back on July 14, he bought "puts"—that is, options to sell—representing the energy sector of the stock market, in the form of a sector SPDR fund. This is one among several indexed funds that track the S&P 500

corporations as divided into nine categories: consumer discretion-
ary, consumer staples, utilities, technology, and so on. Bachus was
betting that the energy sector fund would fall—in other words,
the combined stock prices of energy industry firms in the S&P 500
would go down. (This is what is called selling short.) He started
small, buying $4,500 worth and cashing in the next day, making
close to $1,500 in capital gains.

Ironically, on July 24, Bachus wrote to the Securities and Exchange Commission requesting that it extend an emergency order
intended to curb naked short selling. Some analysts were blam-
ing the high volatility of the crisis on speculators who made short-
term bets on stock prices by shorting them. A "naked short" re-
fers to short-selling a stock without first borrowing it, or ensuring
the ability to borrow it. This is highly risky for the seller, and it
greatly increases the potential amount of short selling, since anyone can do it, whether or not he can afford it, and whether or not
the stock being shorted is even available. Bachus himself was not
guilty of naked short selling; he was always careful to put in play
small amounts of money that he could afford to lose. But naked
short sellers are really just an extreme version of all short sellers,
and he was actively engaged in betting on the markets to fall.

Bachus was neck-deep in crucial financial decision-making at the
highest levels. A few weeks later, he sent a letter to the Financial
Accounting Standards Board, an independent private-sector organization, expressing concerns that proposed accounting changes
might put at risk $10.5 trillion worth of securitized assets. Bachus
wanted to see an end to mark-to-market accounting, in which an
asset or liability is priced based on the current market value, and
instead allow financial institutions and others to price liabilities
based on the value when they are acquired.[9] His position was cer-

tainly defensible, and it shows he was properly active and concerned with the state of financial markets. But he was not exactly disinterested in those markets.

Bachus kept trading. On August 15 and August 22, he bought more than $11,000 worth of SPDR sector option contracts. A few days later, he pocketed more than $5,000 in capital gains because he "guessed" right.

On the evening of September 18, at 7 P.M., Bachus received another private briefing for congressional leaders by Hank Paulson and Federal Reserve Bank Chairman Ben Bernanke about the current state of the economy. They sat around a long table in the office of Nancy Pelosi, then the Speaker of the House. These briefings were secretive. Often, cell phones and Blackberrys had to be surrendered outside the room to avoid leaks.[10]

What Bachus and his colleagues heard behind closed doors was stunning. As Paulson recounts, "Ben [Bernanke] emphasized how the financial crisis could spill into the real economy. As stocks dropped perhaps a further 20 percent, General Motors would go bankrupt, and unemployment would rise . . . if we did nothing." The members of Congress around the table were, in Paulson's words, "ashen-faced."

Bernanke continued, "It is a matter of days before there is a meltdown in the global financial system." Bachus was among those who spoke. According to Paulson, he suggested recapitalizing the banks by buying shares.[11]

The meeting broke up. *The next day*, September 19, Congressman Bachus bought contract options on Proshares Ultra-Short QQQ, an index fund that seeks results that are 200% of the inverse of the Nasdaq 100 index. In other words, he was shorting the market. It was an inexpensive way to bet that the market would fall. He bought options for $7,846 on a day when the Dow Jones Industrial

Average opened at 8,604. A few days later, on September 23, after the market had indeed fallen, he sold the options for over $13,000 and nearly doubled his money.

He continued in this vein, making short-term bets lasting between a day and a week, benefiting on 100-point swings. Meanwhile, the Treasury Department had worked with congressional leaders (including Bachus) to cobble together the $700 billion TARP rescue plan. The plan was publicly announced on September 22. Bachus made another options buy on Proshares Ultra on the day of the announcement. The congressman nearly doubled his money again, bringing in an additional $2,081 in capital gains.

On September 23, the House voted against the bailout as proposed by the Treasury Department. Amendments and revisions were offered. Bachus would later be criticized by his Republican colleagues for waffling on the bill: at first he was for it, then against it, then for it again. As the bill was recast and modified, Bachus's Financial Services Committee continued with private consultations. It was not until October 3 that the revised $700 billion bailout plan passed in the House and was signed into law by President Bush. At the signing ceremony in the Rose Garden of the White House, President Bush praised Bachus's work.

The bill gave the Treasury Department the power to purchase the toxic debt on banks' balance sheets. Paulson and others remained extremely concerned about the financial situation. Bachus was well aware of where things stood, but was apparently confident that the federal bailout would do the trick. He continued trading options, this time buying shares in an index fund known as Powershares QQQ, which tracks one hundred of the largest nonfinancial companies on the Nasdaq exchange. He bought into the fund on more than ten occasions in October, and he purchased options on the S&P 500 index six times. These were "calls"—that is, bets that the market would rise. Not all of Bachus's trades made money. These were still bets, and sometimes he bet wrong.

On October 14, the federal government tapped into the $700 billion provided by the Emergency Economic Stabilization Act. The government took equity positions in banks that chose to participate. *The next day*, Bachus bought more SPDR option contracts and netted a quick $3,400. On October 21, the Federal Reserve announced it would spend $540 billion to purchase short-term debt from money market mutual funds. *The next day*, Bachus bought more than $5,000 worth of options in Market Vectors TRN. Thanks to his purchase of this call, he more than doubled his money.

Bachus was not just buying options based on broad market funds or a sector of the economy. He also bought options on specific companies. On September 8, Hank Paulson received a disturbing private phone call from General Electric CEO Jeffrey Immelt. GE was having trouble selling its bonds, Immelt quietly told him.[12] Just two days later, Bachus bought General Electric call options. He did so four times in a single day, according to his financial statements from Fidelity, and more than doubled his money.[13] Indeed, between September 10 and 15, Bachus traded GE a total of twelve times. Nine of those trades were profitable—a high batting average for such a risky game. Is there absolute proof that Paulson told Bachus about Immelt's phone call? No. Are Bachus's trades suspicious? You bet. Why did he bet so heavily on a company whose business is heavily in financial services?

This was not the only instance when Bachus took leveraged stock options that were intertwined with his government work. Back in 1997, he aggressively purchased eleven put options on United Airlines, betting on the stock to fall. At the time, Bachus was on the House Transportation and Infrastructure Committee, which set policy toward the airlines. That same year, Bachus also took short positions in Microsoft. The Department of Justice was in the midst of its antitrust case against the company. Bachus purchased two puts just days before the Justice Department filed a complaint demanding a $1-million-per-day fine against Microsoft for its violation of a consent decree. Is there proof that he knew about the complaint? No. But the larger pattern is suspicious. In the middle of the antitrust hearings he placed more bets that Microsoft stock would fall. On the Microsoft transactions he netted up to $20,000 in capital gains, according to his financial disclosure form.

Bachus has been able to use his above-average success with option trades to yield a nice supplemental income. In 2007, the congressman undertook several dozen risky short-term put and call options on a variety of companies. He was betting that he would know whether a company's price would go up or down. These included companies like Apple as well as obscure Chinese Internet advertising companies like Focus Media. Bachus had impeccable timing. In over two dozen cases, representing more than two-thirds of all the trades he made, he guessed correctly.

In the case of Focus Media, for example, he held the investment for only two weeks, and sold it on the same day that the company's stock price surged following its announcement that it would acquire a competitor. Again, there is no proof that he knew of the acquisition in advance. But it is highly unlikely that his two-thirds success rate in those 2007 trades could have been based on public information alone. If so, he should have quit Congress and become a professional investor. All told, in 2007 Bachus was able to supplement his $165,200 congressional salary with $160,000 in profits from aggressive put and call options on a variety of stocks.[14]

A spokesman for Bachus, Jeff Emerson, claims that this presented no difficulty. "There is no conflict of interest," he says.

"He asked the Ethics Committee if he could do this, and they said there's no problem." As a matter of law, that answer is accurate and complete. Only Congress's own Ethics Committee can decide whether to condone this kind of stock trading.

Here's the heart of the scandal—the fact that the Ethics Committee deems this acceptable. Welcome to the outrageous arrogance of crony capitalism in Washington. Not only are members of Congress able to act on information that is not available to the rest of us, but they are able to put their own fortunes at risk when they ought to be concerned only with the public interest. If you bet on a particular sector of the economy to fall over the course of a few days or weeks, how can you be sure that your subsequent decisions are not influenced by that bet?

Congressman Bachus was not the only one actively trading stocks while setting policy during the financial crisis. But he was particularly aggressive with options; others merely cashed out of positions that were just about to worsen. Sometimes knowing inside information can mean protecting your assets while the rest of America goes over a financial cliff.

On Tuesday, September 16, 2008, when Henry Paulson and Fed Chairman Ben Bernanke held another of their terrifying closed-door meetings with congressional leaders (two days before the "ashen-faced" meeting), the stock market had dipped only a few percentage points, and most people assumed that the financial crisis was a disruption that would have just a limited effect on the broader economy. But what Paulson and Bernanke told lawmakers on September 16 made it clear that the public's perception was wrong. Paulson, in his memoir, explains that during the meeting he outlined that the federal government was going to bail out the insurance giant AIG and that the markets were in deep trouble.

"There was an almost surreal quality to the meeting," he recounts. "The stunned lawmakers looked at us as if not quite believing what they were hearing."[15]

The next day, Congressman Jim Moran, Democrat of Virginia, a member of the Appropriations Committee, dumped his shares in *ninety* different companies.[16] Moran is a former mayor and city councilman of Alexandria, Virginia. Earlier in his political career he had faced legal charges for casting a vote on the Alexandria City Council that helped a developer friend win a bid for a lucrative plot of land. Moran pleaded no contest to a misdemeanor charge and resigned. It did not stop his career. He was elected mayor in 1985, and to Congress shortly after. (It's interesting to note that legal standards in Virginia are apparently higher than those of the U.S. Congress. Had Moran cast that same vote in Congress, there would be no cause for any charges!)

September 17, 2008, was by far Moran's most active trading day of the year. He dumped shares in Goldman Sachs, General Dynamics, Franklin Resources, Flowserve Corporation, Ecolabs, Edison International, Electronic Arts, DirecTV, Conoco, Procter & Gamble, AT&T, Apple, CVS, Cisco, Chubb, and a dozen more companies. *Moran's timing was impeccable.* He didn't profit very much from these trades, but he avoided the larger losses that the general public would face in a matter of weeks. Moran and his wife actually eked out a net capital gain on these trades.

Moran was just one of many. At least ten U.S. senators, including John Kerry, Sheldon Whitehouse, and Dick Durbin, traded stock or mutual funds related to the financial industry the following day. Representative Shelley Capito is a Republican from West Virginia who sits with Congressman Bachus on the House Financial Services Committee. She and her husband dumped between $100,000 and $250,000 in Citigroup stock the day after the briefing. According to her financial disclosures, she and her husband somehow managed to accrue capital gains from Citigroup stock transactions made throughout the crisis, as much as $50,000 worth.[17]

Senator Dick Durbin, the Democratic whip and chairman of the Subcommittee on Financial Services and General Government of the Senate Appropriations Committee, attended that September 16 briefing with Paulson and Bernanke. He sold off $73,715 in stock funds the next day. Following the next terrifying closed-door briefing, on September 18, he dumped another $42,000 in stock.[18] By doing so, Durbin joined some colleagues in saving themselves from the sizable losses that less connected investors would experience. The stock market collapsed shortly after these congressional trades. By October 3, just seventeen days after the September 18 meeting, the market had dropped more than 9%. A month later, it had plummeted over 22%. Preventing a catastrophic loss can be just as important as making a big gain.

Senator Durbin did not just sell stocks based on his inside knowledge. Like Bachus, he was looking for opportunities to invest. Though he sold many of his holdings, he also bought tens of thousands of dollars' worth of Berkshire Hathaway, the holding company run by the legendary investor Warren Buffett. Durbin bought shares on September 19 and 22—more than $60,000 worth. His timing was nearly perfect. *The next day*, September 23, it was announced that Berkshire Hathaway was buying part of Goldman Sachs, which would yield a 10% guaranteed dividend for Berkshire investors like Durbin. The deal had been discussed behind closed doors for days before Buffett announced it publicly. Durbin's spokesman insists that the senator "didn't use any information from that closed-door gathering to counsel his trades the following day." Yet it is almost certain that Durbin, as chairman of a crucial subcommittee, knew about the Goldman Sachs deal.

When the House Financial Services Committee was crafting legislation for the TARP bailout of banks in the fall of 2008, eight members of the committee were actively and aggressively trading bank stocks. So too were members of the Senate Finance Committee. As the Treasury Department was conferring over which banks would get the bailout money, Senator John Kerry started buying Citigroup stock. The markets might have been down and in turmoil, but Kerry was buying the troubled company. Lots of it. He purchased up to $550,000 in Citigroup stock in early and mid-October. He also bought up to $350,000 in Bank of America shares. *Days later,* on October 28, it was announced that Citigroup was getting $25 billion from the TARP Capital Purchase Program and another $25 billion from the Targeted Investment Program. On November 4, it was announced that Citi would be provided additional loan guarantees that could total $277 billion, from the Treasury, the Federal Reserve, and the Federal Deposit Insurance Corporation.[19]

Members of Congress are privy to all sorts of inside information about pending government actions. Some of it comes from their actual actions — that is, passing legislation. Some of it comes as a result of their position of power. Legislators are told things by regulators or bureaucrats in private because they ask about them. While a committee's public hearings are generally about stagecraft, very frank and detailed conversations often take place behind closed doors. The most valuable information is revealed in private meetings, phone calls, and correspondence. If members of Congress buy and trade stock based on that information, or if they pass that information along to a campaign contributor or their own financial advisers, they are not considered guilty of any wrongdoing. Yes, this is an outrageous standard. But remember, they write their own rules.

Consider for a moment the fact that the political class regularly trades stock in government-backed entities like Fannie Mae and Freddie Mac while *at the same time* determining the fate of those very entities.

Fannie and Freddie were chartered by Congress, and both have implied government guarantees. For many years, these entities were exempt from the nation's financial disclosure regulations—and politicians traded shares in these companies. Indeed, Fannie and Freddie were even exempt from insider trading rules. And in this murky world, Senate and House members invested with one hand while they exercised oversight with the other.

In February 2003, Rahm Emanuel was a newly elected member of Congress from Chicago. He had a seat on the House Financial Services Committee's Subcommittee on Capital Markets, Insurance, and Government-Sponsored Enterprises, which had direct supervision over Fannie and Freddie. Emanuel had previously served on the Freddie Mac board—he'd been appointed by President Clinton in 2000—so he was very familiar with its inner workings. On February 21, Emanuel suddenly sold off all of his Freddie Mac stock, up to $250,000 worth.[20] He did so *just days* before a nearly 10% drop in the share price. It was not until the late spring that the public learned in full what was going on at Freddie Mac: there was a criminal investigation of its senior executives, and its earnings had been inflated and would need to be restated to the tune of billions of dollars. (The Freddie Mac accounting scandal was actually larger than that of Enron.)

Were a board member or employee with intimate knowledge of a corporation to dump all of his shares right before an announcement of bad news and a plunge in the stock price, it would at least warrant a look by the SEC. But when a member of Congress does the same thing, he gets a free pass.

The profitability and stock price of Fannie and Freddie have been closely tied to the politics of Washington. On Election

WE KNOW WHAT'S HAPPENING BEFORE YOU DO

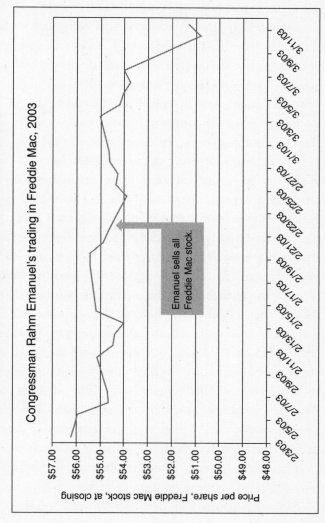

Congressman Rahm Emanuel's trading in Freddie Mac, 2003

Price per share, Freddie Mac stock, at closing

$57.00
$56.00
$55.00
$54.00
$53.00
$52.00
$51.00
$50.00
$49.00
$48.00

2/3/03
2/5/03
2/7/03
2/9/03
2/11/03
2/13/03
2/15/03
2/17/03
2/19/03
2/21/03
2/23/03
2/25/03
2/27/03
3/1/03
3/3/03
3/5/03
3/7/03
3/9/03
3/11/03

Emanuel sells all
Freddie Mac stock.

Day 2004, when exit polls initially—and wrongly, as it turned out—suggested that John Kerry would win the presidency, Fannie Mae stock markedly rose. When it became clear on November 3 that President Bush had been reelected, Fannie stock opened down and fell sharply for the day, while financial stocks gained overall.[21] The reason is simple: George W. Bush was seen as a likely proponent of reforming the government-backed financial giant, whereas Senator Kerry was an opponent of such reforms.

There is nothing wrong or unusual about that stock movement, nor anything surprising about the positions taken by Bush and Kerry on the issue. But were those positions influenced by self-interest? For years, Kerry had been an advocate for expanding Fannie Mae's mission, not reforming it.[22] He was generally opposed to removing any government guarantees, tightening lending standards, or greater regulatory oversight by Congress. As Kerry was resisting legislative efforts to impose additional regulatory restrictions on the financial giant, he and his wife were quietly selling off their extensive Fannie Mae holdings throughout early 2005.[23] Indeed, over a six-month period they dumped around $1 million in Fannie Mae stock. (Again, only ranges were disclosed, not actual figures.) Furthermore, the Kerrys were trading their shares at the same time that the company was telling all of its employees that they could not trade the stock until the new earning results were made public.[24] The Kerrys, who had traded Fannie Mae shares for years, dumped the stock before it suffered serious declines. They actually managed to post capital gains on the stock of up to $250,000 on those transactions.[25] How many other Fannie Mae investors could claim that, in what was a bad time for the stock?

Members of Congress sometimes pay lip service to avoiding potential conflicts of interest. Indeed—and ironically—in 2009, when the federal government was passing out hundreds of billions of dollars in TARP funds to private financial institutions, Speaker of the House Nancy Pelosi argued that "when there's been a thought of conflict of interest" between a member's financial holdings and government bailouts, then that member "should divest."[26]

But there is simply no evidence that Pelosi, or any other member, did so. And there is no evidence of any member of Congress recusing himself when it came to voting on matters that would directly benefit him.

They bet on their own games. They bet on failure. Is there any solid evidence that their political decisions were tied to these bets?

For that, you have to look at some very narrow, tailored bets. Sometimes legislators receive big financial favors from specific companies — and then they work to help those firms.

3

_____

IPOs: INVEST IN POLITICIANS OFTEN

I F YOU COME into Congress already rich, serving there will give you an opportunity to become even richer.

In early 2008, Speaker of the House Nancy Pelosi and her husband, Paul, placed a very big bet. On March 18, the Pelosis made the first of three purchases of Visa stock, totaling between $1 million and $5 million.[1] But this was no ordinary stock transaction. Somehow the Pelosis managed to get their hands on shares of what would become one of the most popular and lucrative initial public offerings of stock in American history. An IPO, as the name implies, is the first stock offering made by a company prior to its going public. Visa had been privately held by a group of banks up until that year.

Mere mortals would have to wait until March 19, when the stock would be publicly traded, to get their shares. According to the Pelosis' financial disclosures, two of their purchases were made after the nineteenth, but one was made before. They listed all three purchases together on their disclosure statement, making it impossible to know how many shares they purchased in the initial offering.

In any event, getting access to this IPO was virtually impossible for the average individual investor. MarketWatch and other news organizations reported that the IPO was "oversubscribed." In the words of IPO analyst Scott Sweet, it was drawing "extreme demand." Virtually all of the Visa IPO shares were going to institutional investors, or large mutual funds or pension funds. Renaissance Capital declared the offering to be the "IPO of the year."[2] Who got these coveted shares? Only "special customers," handpicked investors, received the IPO shares at the opening price of $44. Two days later, after public trading began, the stock price jumped to $65 a share. In short, the Pelosis made a 50% profit on their investment in a matter of two days. They liked the stock so much, they made another purchase, on March 25. On June 4, 2008, they made a third purchase—and Visa stock closed at $85 a share.

What makes this all the more remarkable is that this single investment represented at least 10% of the Pelosis' stock portfolio and potentially as much as half of their equity holdings (depending on where in the range of $1 million to $5 million it actually fell). They were staking a good part of their fortune on one company. How unusual was this for the Pelosis? Although rich in real estate, according to their financial disclosure form, they had only once before committed more than $1 million of their assets to a large, publicly traded corporation: Apple Computer.

It was an enormous risk. Or was it?

The Speaker of the House and her husband just happened to get those IPO shares barely two weeks after a threatening piece of legislation for Visa was introduced in the House of Representatives. John Conyers, chairman of the House Judiciary Committee and an old liberal warhorse, was joined by conservative Republicans Chris Cannon of Utah and Steve King of Iowa, among others, in introducing the Credit Card Fair Fee Act of 2008. The bill had forty-five sponsors in all. It would effectively allow retailers to negotiate lower fees with Visa and the other credit card companies. Retailers argued that these companies—American Express, Visa, MasterCard, and Discover—often set fees together, like a cartel.

By way of background, it's important to understand that Visa does not issue credit cards or make loans; banks do. Visa makes its money by licensing the Visa name and through something called an interchange fee. Every time you use a card at a store, the merchant pays Visa an interchange fee, somewhere between 1% and 3%. Merchants argued that Visa, MasterCard, American Express, and Discover should not be able to keep their fees so high. The Credit Card Fair Fee Act would have amended antitrust laws to require the card companies to enter negotiations with merchants over their interchange fees, and if they could not agree on fees, the Justice Department and the Federal Trade Commission would be empowered to arbitrate. These fees are a huge source of revenue for Visa and the other credit card companies, and a constant thorn in the side of merchants. In 2008, the four companies took in $48 billion in revenue, or about $427 per household, from interchange fees.[3]

Needless to say, Visa and the others were adamantly opposed to the legislation. It was a very "bad bill," in the words of Visa's general counsel.[4]

One would think that this piece of legislation would appeal to Pelosi. She had been outspoken about antitrust problems posed by insurance, oil, and pharmaceutical companies. And she was vocal about the need for controlling the interest rates individual banks charged to use their credit cards. This particular bill had grown out of a House Judiciary Committee Antitrust Task Force Subcommittee study.[5] Big lobbying groups like the National Retail Federation and the National Grocers Association were strongly in favor of it. Indeed, the Maplight Foundation looked at the campaign contributors pushing for this bill on both sides of the aisle and found that Pelosi received twice as many contributions from supporters than from opponents. On top of that, the bill was popular with the public, too. One survey revealed that a whopping 77% of voters were in favor of its passage.[6]

In fact, the bill did pass in the Judiciary Committee on a 19–16 vote, with yeas from 10 Democrats and 9 Republicans. Supporters of the bill were excited. "There is certainly time for the bill to reach a vote before the full House before the end of the year," said one. It was only mid-July.[7]

The National Association of Convenience Stores lobbied for a vote. "It is imperative to tell your Representative to request a vote on the House Floor from Nancy Pelosi," the association wrote to its members. Supporters of the bill waited. And waited. And waited. Speaker Pelosi made sure it never got a hearing on the House floor.

Around the same time, Congressman Peter Welch of Vermont introduced a second bill on interchange fees. Called the Credit Card Interchange Fee Act of 2008, it did not go as far as the Credit Card Fair Fee Act. Welch's bill was merely a call for transparency: it would require the credit card firms to let consumers know how much they were paying in interchange fees. Again, Visa was adamantly opposed. This second bill suffered the same fate as the first, never making it to the House floor.

The following year, both bills were reintroduced. Conyers's bill, now called the Credit Card Fair Fee Act of 2009, had even more support this time, including among conservative Republicans like Joe Barton of Texas and liberals like Zoe Lofgren of California. Welch reintroduced his bill as well. Yet again, neither made it to the House floor.

To be sure, Speaker Pelosi did champion a credit card reform bill, one that did become law, but it focused on interest rates charged by the banks. The Credit Card Reform Act provided consumers more information about credit card fees and prevented the issuers of credit cards from jacking up rates. Pelosi declared, on November 4, 2009, that the Credit Card Reform Act was a great victory. "Today, the House voted overwhelmingly to send a strong and clear message to credit card companies; we will hold you accountable for your anti-consumer practices," she said.[8] None of this affected Visa, however, only its client banks. Interchange fees were not touched, though the bill contained a vague clause stating that the issue should be "studied." Little surprise, then, that Visa stock went up when the bill passed. Having squelched legislative action on interchange fees for more than two years, Speaker Pelosi and her husband saw their Visa stock climb in value. The IPO shares they had purchased soared by 203% from where they began, while the stock market as a whole was down 15% during the same period. Isn't crony capitalism beautiful?

Congress did eventually act to deal with credit card swipe fees. But Speaker of the House Pelosi had little to do with it. The Frank-Dodd Wall Street Reform and Consumer Protection Act included a clause that required the Federal Reserve Bank to study and take action on the matter. Pelosi was pushed by her colleagues to support these efforts, but remained outside the fray.[9]

All too often we think of corporate interests in terms of campaign contributions or lobbyists. There is a more direct path for corporations and executives to advance their interests: help politicians get rich.

Companies recognize the importance of having friends in

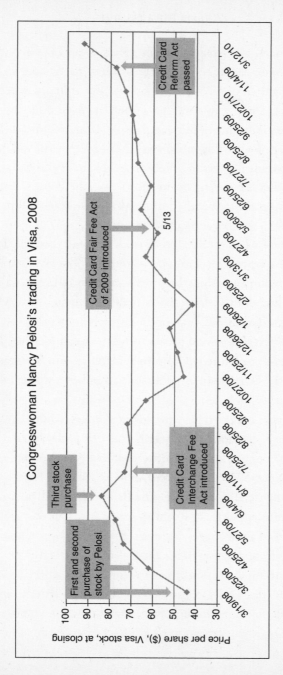

PROTECTING OUR INVESTMENT

Congresswoman Nancy Pelosi's trading in Visa, 2008

powerful places, and granting them access to an IPO is one way to reward them. Members of Congress often participate in IPOs that are difficult, if not close to impossible, for ordinary Americans to join. Pelosi and her husband have been involved in no less than *ten* lucrative IPOs during her congressional career. Not all IPOs, of course, are beyond the public's reach. And some are available by auction, theoretically making them accessible to everyone (assuming your broker is handling the auction). Still, the Pelosis' track record for IPO participation is impressive. These transactions have played a role in making the Pelosis wealthy.

Often the Pelosis received stock in an IPO and then sold it days later for a huge profit. In 1993, they bought IPO shares in Gupta, a high-tech company. After the price soared 88%, they sold it the next day. They did the same when they participated in IPOs involving Netscape and UUNet, both of which doubled in value the same day. They also gained access to other oversubscribed IPOs, including those of Remedy Corporate, Opal, Legato Systems, and Act Networks. They sold all of them within a month or two for hefty profits.

The Pelosis may well have participated in even more IPOs, but Nancy Pelosi's financial disclosure forms often obscure dates on which they bought stocks. In December 1999, for example, they bought between $250,000 and $500,000 worth of stock in a high-tech company called OnDisplay. The Pelosis don't tell you exactly *when* they got the shares; they simply list "2X various dates" for the transactions on the congresswoman's disclosure form. OnDisplay went public in mid-December of that year, so the purchases must have happened in that month. And the investment worked out very well. *Months later,* OnDisplay was bought out by Vignette, and the Pelosis made up to $1 million in capital gains. Interestingly, Vignette's IPO was underwritten by William Hambrecht, an investment banker, a longtime friend of Nancy Pelosi's, and a major campaign contributor.

A few years later, the same Bill Hambrecht went before the House Finance Committee, chaired by Barney Frank, a Pelosi ally, to push for a change in the registration process for stock IPOs, an exemption called Regulation A. Under current law, a company that plans an IPO of less than $5 million in stock gets an exemption from detailed reporting. Hambrecht wanted the exemption raised to $30 million, which would greatly benefit his business, making IPOs easier, quicker, and far less expensive. As the hearings began, Congressman Frank said, "I should note also that it was Speaker Pelosi who first called this to our attention earlier in the year. It is something that the speaker has taken a great interest in because of her interest in job creation, so we have had to find a way to have this hearing."[10] Indeed!

Pelosi is not alone in benefiting from IPOs. Other lawmakers have profited from public offerings issued by companies and entities interested in currying favor in Washington. Senator Robert Torricelli, for example, made $70,000 in one day, courtesy of a New Jersey bank's IPO. In 1997 alone, Torricelli was involved in no fewer than nine stock IPOs. Senator Jeff Bingaman enjoyed a 378% return on his investment in Avanex after just one day of trading. Senator Barbara Boxer reaped rich returns after she was given the chance to participate in IPOs involving Avenue A (up 200% the first day) and Interwave Communications (up 184%).[11] There are no doubt many other lawmakers who have participated in IPOs, but they are not required to designate their stock transactions as such. And it is extremely difficult to track IPO transactions given to politicians.

Congressman Gary Ackerman was given access to stock in a

private company—and he didn't even need to use his own money to make a large profit. Ackerman, who sits on the Financial Services Committee, had the opportunity in 2002 to buy private shares in a company called Xenonics, which makes military-related technologies. The investment didn't cost Ackerman one cent. The firm's biggest shareholder, Selig Zises, loaned the congressman $14,000 to buy the stock. "Gary is one of my closest friends," explained Mr. Zises. "I was only happy for Gary to make some money. If the thing succeeded, he paid me back."[12]

Ackerman used his position as a congressman, and as a fervent supporter of Israel, to arrange a meeting between Xenonics executives and Israeli officials to discuss a deal involving the company's night-vision systems. After the company went public in 2005, Ackerman was able to sell his shares for more than $100,000.[13]

Did Ackerman do anything wrong? Most of us would say yes! But experts say that based on current rules, the only thing he did wrong was not have a written agreement covering the loan. Otherwise, it was all aboveboard—at least according to House ethics rules. Think of it: you can get IPO shares in a company, buy them with money from a friend, make lots of money, and your only mistake is not writing the loan down on paper.[14]

Other members of Congress could be singled out too. But Nancy Pelosi stands out for two reasons: not only is she enormously wealthy, and thus (like John Kerry) able to invest in large amounts, she is also one of the highest-ranking members of the House. There are many companies that want to curry favor with the Speaker or majority leader of the House of Representatives.

One of the IPOs that the Pelosis participated in was Clean Energy Fuels, in which they landed up to $100,000 of stock. The company was founded by Texas billionaire T. Boone Pickens, who wanted to promote the use of liquid natural gas as a solution to America's dependence on foreign energy. In other words, the company was hoping to exploit America's vast natural gas reserves while reducing our dependence on petroleum. Arguably, that's a fine goal. As the *Wall Street Journal* noted at the time, expanding natural gas was a key plank of the Democratic Party's energy platform.[15] What isn't so fine is that the Pelosis now had a financial stake in the issue. As Speaker, Nancy Pelosi pushed a series of bills that would benefit Clean Energy Fuels. The stock did well. The Pelosis got it at around $12 a share. By April 2010, it was trading at more than $20 a share.

The Pelosis' investment in natural gas did not end there. In November 2007, they participated in yet another IPO, this one involving Quest Energy Partners. They bought up to $500,000 in what was described by investment advisers as "a company that exploits and develops natural gas properties." (This IPO was handled by Wachovia Securities.)[16]

Pelosi became a champion of natural gas, pushing for tax benefits as well as aggressively backing global warming legislation that would tax carbon emissions. Natural gas would benefit enormously if any of these bills became law. Pelosi went so far as to state on *Meet the Press*, "I believe in natural gas as a clean, cheap alternative to fossil fuels." (Of course, natural gas *is* a fossil fuel.) There is nothing wrong with a policy decision to reduce our dependence on foreign oil. But there is something wrong when the policymaker has a financial stake in the game.

In 2008, Clean Energy Fuels also backed California Proposition 10, a ballot initiative that would require the state to float a $5 billion bond offering to subsidize the purchase of "alternative fuel" vehicles. Clean Energy Fuels donated at least $3.2 million to the ballot campaign. Nancy Pelosi endorsed the initiative.

In corporate America this would be a clear conflict of interest. Persuading a corporation to spend money on an initiative that you as an executive would personally profit from would raise huge questions. And if you were a middle-level employee in the executive branch of government, such a conflict of interest would trigger an investigation. Trying to help companies in which you have a large financial stake become more profitable through congressional legislation *is the very definition of conflict of interest*. But Pelosi tried to turn what was a vice for most everyone else into a virtue. "I'm investing in something I believe in," she told *Meet the Press* host Tom Brokaw. "I believe in natural gas as a clean, cheap alternative to fossil fuel." But, of course, she was also investing in something she could make more profitable by changing government policy. When Brokaw asked her that very question, she responded, "That's the marketplace."[17]

But it's a marketplace where politicians get to set the terms and the rules and influence the outcome. Accumulating wealth or growing the wealth you already have is much easier when you have a piece of the action.

4

THIS LAND IS MY LAND

R ECALL THE STORY that opened this book, of Dennis Hastert's $10 million gain during his speakership. Unlike many of his colleagues, Hastert was never much of a stock trader. So how exactly did he do it?

By following George Washington Plunkitt's lead, in the form of a land deal. For Plunkitt, this entailed buying up land that he knew the government would need to purchase in the not too distant future and then selling it to the government for a healthy profit. Today, such a blatant move would appear too crude. Yet the land deal survives in disguised form. The Permanent Political Class has become more sophisticated in how it enriches itself by mixing real estate investments with taxpayer money. It is completely legal. Indeed, congressional ethics committees have even deemed it "ethical." And land deals are easier to camouflage than stock transactions. You can be fuzzy about the location of the property, and since there is no set price for the land, as there is for shares of stock, you can mask your profits more easily.

In 2002, Hastert bought a 195-acre farm on Little Rock Creek, in Kendall County, Illinois. He purchased it in July, just before the state's transportation secretary, Kirk Brown, approved the design of a land corridor for a road called the Prairie Parkway, on July 31. The farm was just 2.4 miles from the parkway corridor and 5 miles from the nearest proposed highway interchange. In February 2004, Hastert and two partners made a second land purchase. They formed a trust and bought another 69 acres right by the interchange in Plano, Illinois. They paid $15,000 an acre. Hastert reported this on his financial disclosure form, but his name does not appear on real estate records. Instead, Kendall County public records show that a Little Rock Trust #225 acquired the property. On his disclosure form, Hastert listed the investment simply as "¼ share in 69 acres (Plano, IL.)," giving no address or parcel number, as he is required to do by House rules.

Plano is smack dab in the middle of farm country. It is the birthplace of the mechanical reaper. It boasts a population of about 5,000. It's also the town where Hastert has maintained his residence. As farmland those 69 acres were of some value. But as a possible residential site, where the land could be split up and developed, the sky was the limit. And that's what was intended: the Robert Arthur Land Company, through an entity called RALC Plano, was developing a residential community called North County, which would include more than 1,600 acres of land (including Hastert's acreage) as well as 33 acres of commercial enterprises and retail shops. In addition, 18 acres were set aside for a public school.

To create such a large residential community in a rural area, you need roads. Wide roads. The Kendall County Board had al-

WE BUILD THE SPEAKER OF THE HOUSE A ROAD

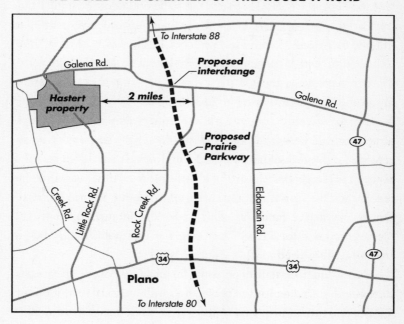

ready approved the construction of an interchange on nearby Glena Road. But someone had to pay for it.

Two months after Speaker Hastert purchased his share in the land, the most powerful man in Congress inserted a $207 million earmark into the federal highway bill to begin building on the Prairie Parkway. An earmark is a way for members of Congress to get money for specific, often local projects. In the words of the White House Office of Management and Budget, it's a way that "circumvents otherwise applicable merit-based or competitive allocation processes" to make favored projects happen.[1]

Apparently not content with just a quarter share of 69 acres, a few months later (May 2, 2005) Hastert and his wife transferred an additional 69 acres of land to the Little Rock Trust. Seven months after that (December 7, 2005), a little more than a year after he made the first Plano land purchase, and with the Prairie Parkway in the works, the land was sold for $4.9 million. Land that had been purchased for $15,000 per acre was now sold for $36,000 a acre—a 140% profit.

According to Hastert's personal financial disclosure, these sales amounted to transactions of between $2 million and $10 million for his personal stake. Not a bad return for a short-term investment.[2]

You and I as taxpayers helped Hastert become wealthy. Involuntarily, of course.

Imagine for a moment that Hastert was not a member of the political class but instead was a corporate executive or a school superintendent. What would happen if he used corporate or county assets in a way that would personally benefit his real estate holdings? If discovered, he would at a minimum get fired. He might even be sued, or charged with criminal fraud. But what Hastert did as a politician is common among the political class.

Members of Congress have used federal earmarks to enhance the value of their own real estate holdings in several ways: by extending a light rail mass transit line near their property, by expanding an airport, or by cleaning up a nearby shoreline. Federal funds have been used to build roads, beautify land, and upgrade neighborhoods near commercial and residential real estate owned by legislators, substantially increasing values and the net worth of our elected officials, courtesy of taxpayer money. Not only is this legal — by the bizarre standards of the Permanent Political Class — it's also deemed "ethical." Congressional ethics rules simply say that as long as a member can demonstrate that at least one other person will benefit from an earmark, that earmark is in the "public interest." Try out that ethical standard at your job and see how it works for you.

Dennis Hastert represented a rural district in Illinois. The Speaker of the House who followed him, Nancy Pelosi, represents urban San Francisco. Unlike Hastert, Pelosi and her husband have a large stock portfolio. But they also have extensive commercial real estate holdings. And like Hastert, Nancy Pelosi has used federal taxpayer money through earmarks to substantially increase the value of those investments.

For years, Nancy Pelosi has pushed for earmarks to construct and ultimately extend San Francisco's so-called Third Street Light Rail Project. In 2004, she boasted to her constituents that she had secured more than $120 million in federal money for the project. Third Street is one of the most expensive light rail projects ever, costing $660 million for just a six-mile route. The light rail system includes distinctive marquee poles with sculptures and mobiles, and new street lighting. The rail line is designed to generate a green light at every intersection so trains can travel smoothly from station to station, stopping traffic along the way.

Phase I of the project was heavily funded by the Federal Transit Administration's New Starts program. Pelosi helped secure the funding, to the tune of $532 million, to get the project under way, and another $200 million to continue construction and begin planning for phase two of the project. For the initial $532 million, she actually secured "cost-effectiveness exemptions" from the federal government to make the deal possible. In 2008, she got an additional $11.7 million to help finance Phase II, and over the course of three years she set aside $28 million more for it.[3]

The new transit line serves as a "key infrastructure improvement to help support revitalization of communities along the corridor," in the words of the San Francisco metro authority. Interestingly enough, that happens to include one of Nancy Pelosi's most valuable real estate assets.[4]

Pelosi and her husband own a four-story office building at 45 Belden Place. The building is worth between $1 million and $5 million, according to their financial disclosure. Paul Pelosi receives a management fee for handling the property (which he is not required to disclose) on top of net rent of between $100,000 and $1 million per year.

Phase II of the Third Street project runs just two blocks from the Pelosis' commercial buildings. Two stops on the line—Chinatown and Union Square/Market Square—are three blocks from the Pelosis' buildings. Why does this matter? Realtors have a name for it: "transit premium." The National Association of Realtors says that high-quality mass transit (like this project) can increase property values by "over 150 percent." A $3 million commercial building can become a $7 million building practically overnight.

According to a study by the association, location is key: you don't want the metro stop to be too close or too far. There's a sweet spot for obtaining the maximum transit premium: two to four blocks away is ideal.[5]

Another study by two academics found that a light rail system in Santa Clara County, California, boosted commercial real estate values by 120%.[6]

WE BUILD ANOTHER SPEAKER A LIGHT RAIL SYSTEM

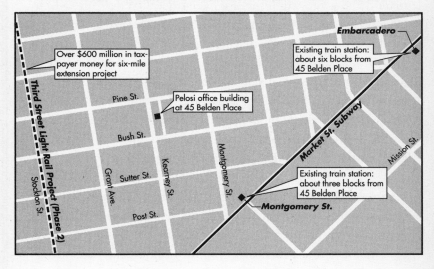

Nancy Pelosi seems to have a history of advancing earmarks that are near her family's commercial real estate. (Actually, Pelosi doesn't like to use the word "earmark." At a 2007 press conference she said, "Why don't we leave here today forgetting the word earmark?" She suggested the phrase "legislative directive" instead.) In 2005, Pelosi pushed for another $20 million earmark, for waterfront redevelopment only two blocks away from the Belden Street property. The earmark was killed in July of that year. The Pelosis increased their financial stake in the property, and the next year Pelosi asked for the earmark again, and this time she succeeded.[7] On another occasion she secured $12 million for the beautification of Geary Boulevard in San Francisco, which happens to abut an investment property the Pelosis own on Point Lobos Avenue.

Nancy Pelosi is not the only elected official who earmarked a mass transit project that was in close proximity to real estate holdings and apparently profited handsomely from it. Congresswoman Carolyn Maloney represents parts of Queens and Manhattan, including the Upper East Side "silk stocking district." A former member of the New York City Council, Maloney was first elected to Congress in 1992. For many years she was married to an investment banker, Clifton Maloney, until he passed away in 2009.

In 2007, Congresswoman Maloney, together with New York Senators Charles Schumer and Hillary Clinton, secured an earmark of $167 million for a new MTA subway line. In 2009, she helped obtain another $277 million for the project. In 2010, a third earmark, for $197 million, was approved. The long-sought-after Second Avenue subway, running up the East Side of Manhattan, could finally begin construction. It will likely take years to complete, at a cost running well over $10 billion.

Maloney owns a building at 409 East 92nd Street, valued at between $5 million and $25 million. On her personal financial disclosure, she lists it as a "rental property & residence." Plans for the new subway line feature a stop that happens to be three blocks away from her building—again, right in the "sweet spot."

Congressman Mike Thompson of California inserted into the 2010 federal budget an earmark to expand a small regional airport in his district.[8] Thompson's earmark was for $280,000 to upgrade the Napa Valley, California, airport—specifically, for a "runway 36L glidescope."

As it happens, the Pelosis own a vineyard and home in St. Helena, California, worth between $5 million and $25 million, and another property nearby. They also own a stake in an exclusive resort called Auberge du Soleil in Rutherford, worth between $1 million and $5 million. All of these properties are *north* of the airport, sitting beneath what had been the flight path for planes coming in to land. But with the new glideslope, according to the airport, more planes would be able to approach from the south. The Pelosi properties would be spared from overhead noise.[9]

Funding for the expansion of the Napa Valley airport by Thompson's earmark is not the only earmark that has benefited Pelosi's personal investments. Also in 2008, an earmark was inserted in the federal highway bill to widen and improve an exit ramp on California's historic Highway 101. That might not strike anyone as unusual, except for the fact that the interchange is *next to* a shopping mall owned by Pelosi and her husband. According to her financial disclosure forms, that mall brings in between $100,000 and $1 million a year in net income.

So why did legislators do Pelosi a favor? She is the most powerful Democrat in the House. If you want to get something done, it needs to go through her.

The earmark game is bipartisan. Republican Senator Judd Gregg of New Hampshire, whose father, Hugh Gregg, served as governor and was long active in the New Hampshire Republican Party, has spent the bulk of his adult life in political office. Judd was first elected to Congress in 1980, elected governor in 1988, and to the U.S. Senate in 1992. A little more than a decade after joining the Senate, he became chairman of the powerful Budget Committee. In a show of bipartisanship, President Obama tried to nominate Gregg to be his secretary of commerce in 2009. Gregg first accepted, then withdrew, deciding instead to stay in the Senate. He retired in 2010.

Judd Gregg had a reputation as a fiscal conservative, but he was always fond of earmarks. He obtained $266 million in research and development money for the University of New Hampshire, for example, and the school generously named its new technology center Gregg Hall.[10]

While he served as chairman of the powerful Senate Budget Committee, Gregg earmarked some $66 million in taxpayer money to transform Pease Air Force Base in Portsmouth, New Hampshire, into a business park. He managed to secure $24.8 million for a new federal building there, and at least $24.5 million for New Hampshire National Guard projects at the base, including a new fire and crash rescue station. In addition, he garnered almost $9 million for a new wing headquarters, and $8 million to transform the base from military to civilian use, including buying snow-removal equipment and building a parking lot. For good measure, he was able to pull down $475,000 for structures to shield office buildings at the base from airplane and other noises.

Did I mention that Senator Gregg's brother, Cyrus, happened to be the developer of the air base? Or that Senator Gregg himself had invested between $450,000 and $1 million of his own money in what is now called the Pease International Tradeport? Along the way, the senator has collected between $240,000 and $650,000 on his investment. (Curiously, like Hastert, Gregg did not list all of the real estate addresses on his financial disclosure forms.)[11]

Before he secured the earmarks, Gregg invested through several partnerships, including 222 International Drive, LLP, and Say Pease, LLC. The former, for the development of a commercial building, was valued at around $11 million.[12]

When President Obama announced then-Senator Gregg as his choice for commerce secretary in 2009, Gregg was asked about the earmarks and how he profited from them. "I am absolutely sure that in every way I've complied with the ethics rules of the Senate both literally and in their spirit relative to any investment that I've made anywhere," he stated to the press. Unfortunately, he is correct—and that, of course, is the problem: this stuff is *completely legal* and, according to Senate rules, *ethical*. When he made that statement, he should have stopped right there. Instead, he continued: "These earmarks do not benefit me in any way, shape, or manner financially, personally or in any other manner other than the fact that I'm a citizen of New Hampshire."[13] Yeah, sure.

Redeveloping a military base using taxpayer money to boost your investment is of course a benefit, personal and financial: Gregg was able to put his thumb on the scale of fair-market reward for his investment. The former senator now works for Goldman Sachs as a consultant, where he provides "strategic advice" and assists "in business development initiatives."[14]

These kinds of deals are not at all uncommon. Congressman Ken Calvert of California is a Republican member of the powerful Appropriations Committee and was first elected to Congress in 1992. His background is in real estate, and through a real estate firm he partly owns, run by his brother Quint, he is still an active investor.

In 2005, Calvert and a partner paid $550,000 for a 4.3-acre parcel of land just south of March Air Reserve Base in Southern California. Shortly afterward, he secured $1.5 million in taxpayer money to support commercial development around the base. Less than a year after the earmark, Calvert and his partner sold the land (without having made any improvements) for $985,000—a 79% profit. Not bad!

In the early summer of 2005, Calvert's real estate firm brokered a sale involving a property at 20330 Temescal Canyon Road, in Corona, California, which was a few blocks from a proposed interchange for Interstate 15. Calvert then helped secure an earmark to build the interchange. Within six months, the property was sold at a nearly $500,000 profit. Calvert's firm received a commission on both transactions. Good work if you can get it.

Calvert was careful: he sent both of these earmarks to the House Ethics Committee for approval, because he stood to benefit personally from them. The committee, in a letter signed by Congresswoman Stephanie Tubbs Jones and Congressman Alcee Hastings, said the use of taxpayer money was fine because any profits "resulting from the earmark would be incremental and indirect and would be experienced as a member of a class of landholders." In other words, Calvert was not the sole beneficiary, and the earmarked funds were not paid directly to him. [15]

Congressman David Hobson of Ohio helped obtain federal earmarks to build a freight transfer center at the Columbus airport to help ship goods to and from central Ohio. The trouble is that Hobson co-owned an office building near the project, and his tenants included freight companies such as FedEx that would use the freight center. He'd bought the building in 2001, and over the next seven years secured $30 million in federal transportation money to build the freight terminal, which was part of the conversion of old Rickenbacker Air Force Base outside Columbus. On another occasion, in 2004, Hobson worked to get nearly $2 million in taxpayer money to widen a road near Dayton, which happened to run right in front of a condominium development in which he was an investor. He had bought into the project only one year earlier.

Hobson retired from office in 2008. The House Ethics Committee, at the time chaired by Congresswoman Stephanie Tubbs Jones, again said that the earmarks were acceptable because they were only an indirect benefit to Hobson and the airport investment was "speculative."

Congressman Heath Shuler of North Carolina is relatively new to Congress, but he quickly demonstrated his understanding that the power of his position could be helpful in a real estate transaction—particularly if it involved a deal with a government agency that he helped oversee.

First elected in 2006 in a western North Carolina district, Shuler had been a star quarterback at the University of Tennessee who'd had a brief stint in the NFL before becoming a real estate investor. One of his largest holdings in 2007 was in a real estate entity called the Cove at Blackberry Ridge, whose investors owned a large plot of land. According to Shuler's financial disclosures, his stake in the Cove was worth between $5 million and $25 million at the time. The investors planned to turn their land into a residential development. But there was one problem: they didn't have water access rights.

That seemed to be fixed in August 2008 when the Tennessee Valley Authority (TVA) announced a new water access deal for the investment group, providing 145 feet of frontage along the shoreline of the Watts Bar Reservoir in exchange for water access rights the group held in a neighboring county. What makes this so interesting is that at the time Shuler sat on the congressional subcommittee that had oversight of the TVA. When the deal was announced, eyebrows were raised. TVA employees first claimed they did not know Congressman Shuler was involved in the project. For his part, Shuler denied having any contact with the government agency. But later, he admitted that he had indeed picked up the phone and called TVA President Tom Kilgore in 2007 about getting the land-swap deal done. A TVA inspector general's report noted that there was an "inherent conflict of interest" in the swap. The report also said that Shuler's deal "created the appearance of preferential treatment." However, the report was quick to beg off any condemnation. "We make no judgment as to whether Congressman Shuler's actions connected to the Blackberry Cove matter violate any ethical standard." For its part, the House Ethics Committee again found nothing wrong.[16]

Congressman Bennie Thompson, when he is not inserting earmarks for Napa Valley, California, has done so for tiny Bolton, Mississippi, population 600. One earmark was for a museum project; another, for $500,000, was to help improve the infrastructure of the Bolton Industrial Park. What Thompson hopes we don't notice is that he owns commercial real estate in the town, including lots 1, 3, and 31 on L. C. Turner Circle and what he describes as "2 acres of unimproved land in Bolton, Mississippi." It so happens that the earmarked projects are very near his investment properties.

Representative Maurice Hinchey of New York has the honor of being one of the fastest climbers in Congress in terms of net worth. In 2004, his net assets, based on his personal financial disclosure forms, totaled around $74,000. In 2008, he reported an average net worth of $727,000.[17] That's an 800% increase in just four years. How did he do it?

Much of it came through his sponsorship of an earmark for $800,000 to the Department of the Interior for water and wastewater infrastructure improvements in the Hudson Valley town of Saugerties. Specifically, it was for upgrades to Partition Street. In a press release, Hinchey took credit for bringing money to the town: "Congressman Used Position on House Appropriations Subcommittee on Interior to Obtain Funds, Which Will Help Promote Economic Growth in the Village," it read. In the release he boasted that "a second portion of the sanitary system on Route 9W or Partition Street is in the center of the business district of the Village of Saugerties."

What Hinchey didn't mention was that he owned a quarter of the land that sits under the Partition Street project, which calls for the development of a three-story, thirty-room boutique hotel with a restaurant and catering hall.

Hinchey had bought two lots there in 2004 for a combined value of between $30,000 and $100,000. As the earmarked project got under way, the value of his properties surged to *more than five times* their original value. By the time of his 2009 financial disclosure, he listed their value as between $250,000 and $500,000. Incredulously, when asked about the project and the earmark, Hinchey said it was not a conflict of interest. He merely owns the land, he said, and has no direct involvement in the development of the property.[18] Okay. That explains it.

Sometimes members of the Permanent Political Class can enhance the value of their real estate by using a third party. Congressman Jerry Lewis of California has served in the House since 1979, representing three different Southern California districts in the course of three decades (thanks to redistricting). The Republican was chairman of the House Appropriations Committee and is now a senior member of that committee.

Over the past ten years, Lewis has pushed earmarks for a private company called Environmental Systems Research Institute, to the tune of tens of millions of dollars. The firm is based in Redlands, California, and was founded by Jack and Laura Dangermond, who are campaign contributors of Lewis's. In 2001, after receiving the benefits of numerous earmarks from Lewis, the Dangermonds decided to donate 41 pristine acres of land directly across from Lewis's house as part of a scenic canyon. The donation was made to the city of Redlands, and was contingent on its never being developed. Naturally, that gift increased the property value of Lewis's home.[19] In another instance, Lewis secured a $500,000 earmark to upgrade the Barracks Row section of Capitol Hill in Washington. (Some of that money was used to plant flowers.) On the House floor, Lewis explained that he was a firm supporter of beautifying that area. What he never mentioned was that he and his wife owned a $1 million house four blocks away.[20]

Another one of those politicians who has seen his wealth rise in recent years is Senate Majority Leader Harry Reid of Nevada. Reid doesn't trade a lot of stocks, but he does buy and trade land. And he is often able to boost the profits from his investments by the use of the power of his office. In 2005, Senator Reid sponsored an $18 million earmark to build a bridge over the Colorado River to connect Laughlin, Nevada, with Bullhead City, Arizona. (There was already one bridge connecting the two places.) Neighboring Arizona's two senators denounced the earmark as pork, and a completely unnecessary expenditure.

As it happened, a few miles from the proposed bridge there was a 160-acre parcel of land owned by, well, Harry Reid. Local officials predicted that the bridge would "undoubtedly hike land values in an already-booming commuter town, where specula-

LOCATION, LOCATION, LOCATION

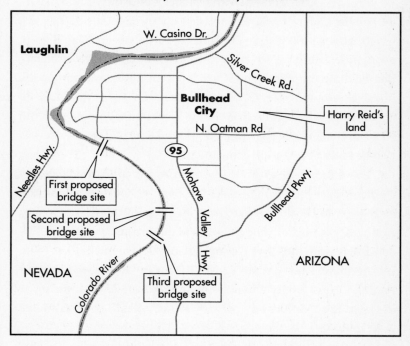

tors are snapping up undeveloped land for housing developments and other projects." Reid's office insisted that "Senator Reid's support for the bridge had absolutely nothing to do with property he owns."[21] Of course.

Reid has done very well with land deals over the years. In 1998, he bought undeveloped residential property just outside Las Vegas for about $400,000. In 2001, he sold it to a friend (Jay Brown, a longtime casino lawyer) for a stake in a limited liability company that held the property. Reid never reported the transaction on his financial disclosure form. By moving the property to the LLC, he could effectively shield it from future disclosures, because now the LLC was technically the owner, not him. All he had to disclose was that he had a stake in the company.

The LLC tried to get the land rezoned from residential to commercial, which would make it far more valuable, submitting its request to the appropriate subcommittee of the Clark County Zoning Commission. The answer was no: rezoning would be "inconsistent" with the Clark County Master Development Plan. (The subcommittee's no vote was 4 to 1.) Brown and Reid then took it to the full Clark County Commission. Reid's name even came up at the hearings. "Mr. Brown's partner is Harry Reid," commissioners were told.

Did I mention that at this time Clark County commissioners were trying to obtain federal earmarks for a variety of projects through Harry Reid's office? Or that Reid had funneled tens of millions of dollars in earmarks to Clark County over the years?

The commission granted the rezoning. Shortly thereafter, Reid and Brown sold the land to a shopping center developer for $1.6 million. Reid's personal take was $1.1 million.[22]

Leveraging your power for a land deal is one of the best paths to honest graft. It's difficult to determine the actual market price of most properties, so disclosure statements can be murky. And when an earmarked project improves the value of the property, it can be hard to calculate just how much that new road, transit stop, or beautification added to it. But there can be little doubt that the political class is the only group of people in America who can get away with using taxpayer money to increase the value of their real estate, while declaring they are doing it in the public's interest.

Part Two

—

CAPITALIST CRONIES

In Part One we looked at the various ways politicians use their power to get rich, or richer than they were when they entered office. The temptation to seize an opportunity—a stock tip, or the power of legislation—is pervasive. But there is a broader, more subtle motivation as well: politicians are surrounded by wealthy friends and donors who use their access to power to enrich themselves. If all of your friends are using you to get rich, wouldn't you want a piece of the action?

In Part Two we will look at the semiprivate sector: businessmen and investors who get rich through their political connections, tilting the playing field of the free market by lobbying for handouts. Just as with the insider trading and land deals in Part One, there is nothing illegal about this aspect of crony capitalism. Unfair, perhaps unethical, perhaps immoral—but not illegal. It would take a revolution in the mindset and the rules of the game in Washington to put a stop to it. But the least we can do is pull back the curtain and bring some sunlight into the dark rooms of the crony game.

5

SPREADING THE WEALTH . . .
TO BILLIONAIRES

God bless the Obama Administration and the U.S. government.
We have really got the A-team now working on green innovation in our country.

— JOHN DOERR, Obama contributor and billionaire investor, who owns a large
stake in sixteen companies that have received government loans or grants

IN *THE AUDACITY OF HOPE*, Barack Obama tells a story about visit-
ing Los Angeles in 2000: His credit card was declined by a rental
car company. It was a "very dry period" for his law firm, and he was
devoting most of his energy to his work as a state senator. Then
suddenly a wealthy political donor named Robert Blackwell agreed
to pay him a $112,000 legal retainer over a fourteen-month period.

But here's what Obama failed to note in his book, and what
came to light only later, thanks to investigative reporting: State
Senator Obama subsequently helped Blackwell's table tennis com-

pany receive $320,000 in Illinois tourism grants to subsidize a state Ping-Pong tournament.[1]

Giving specific access and benefits to those who help you get elected (or get rich through investments) is a time-tested American tradition. You can make a business of government service by helping friends who help you. Politicians have always tried to provide favors in the form of tax breaks, regulatory exemptions, and constituent services to a select group of financial friends. Politicians regularly get special provisions inserted in the tax code to help friends in certain industries. Or they try to get them access to particularly powerful bureaucrats. But the best form of payoff and patronage for rich friends and supporters? *Give them billions of dollars in taxpayer cash.*

When William "Boss" Tweed ran the Tammany Hall political machine in New York City in the nineteenth century, he forced potential candidates to put up cash to win nomination (and then certain election) to office. Once the electees arrived, they would enrich themselves, but they also funneled money back to Tammany Hall. It was more than just crony capitalism; it was also a system of rigged elections. What brought Tweed down, however, was classic cronyism. He began to construct a courthouse in lower Manhattan in 1861, siphoning off several times its value in government contracts. Finally, a *New York Times* investigative series pointed out so much blatant graft—one Tweed crony was paid so much for just two days of work that he became known as "the Prince of Plasterers"—that charges were brought, and Tweed was jailed after milking the courthouse for a decade (construction would not be completed until 1880).

The game of funneling taxpayer money to friends has exploded to astonishing levels in recent years. Now that annual federal outlays exceed $3 trillion, there are extraordinary opportunities to get a piece of the action. Government checks routinely find their way to very wealthy Americans. Convincing the public that billionaires need the money can, needless to say, be tricky. But if a government check somehow serves the "public interest," it can become part of a larger program and might escape scrutiny.

With the dramatic events surrounding the 2008 financial crisis, beginning in 2009 the United States embarked on the greatest reverse–Robin Hood transfer of wealth in its history. Tax money was taken from all, rich and poor, and given to billionaires. Under the guise of an economic stimulus plan to create jobs and to develop alternative energy, Washington has handed out billions of dollars in cash and federal loan guarantees. With the exception of some reports on the solar power company Solyndra, almost entirely unreported by the media is the fact that an overwhelming amount of this money has been directed to wealthy financial backers of President Obama and the Democratic Party. This is Boss Tweed's financial payoffs writ large. Many recipients served on the President's campaign finance committee, or functioned as campaign donation "bundlers" (coordinators of individual contributions that can be combined into large gifts), or were major contributors themselves. In short, they raised and donated *millions* for Obama's 2008 campaign, and in return, the companies they own or lead have received *billions* in government-backed loans and outright grants. (The cash grants, by the way, are tax free.)[2]

When President-elect Obama came to Washington in late 2008 following his electoral victory, he was outspoken about the need for an economic stimulus to revive a struggling economy. He wanted billions of dollars spent on "shovel-ready projects" to build roads; billions more for developing alternative energy projects; and additional billions for expanding broadband Internet access and creating a "smart grid" for energy consumption. After he was sworn in as President, he proclaimed that the allocation of tax-payer money would be based strictly on merit—not doled out to political friends. "Decisions about how Recovery Act dollars are spent will be based on the merits," he said, referring to the American Recovery and Reinvestment Act of 2009. "Let me repeat that: Decisions about how Recovery money will be spent will be based on the merits. They will not be made as a way of doing favors for lobbyists."[3]

Really? Let's look at the results.

It would take an entire book to analyze every single grant and government-backed loan doled out since Barack Obama became President. But an examination of grants and guaranteed loans offered by just one stimulus program run by the Department of Energy, for alternative energy projects, is stunning. The so-called 1705 Loan Guarantee Program and the 1603 Grant Program channeled billions of dollars to all sorts of energy companies. The grants were earmarked for alternative fuel and green-power projects, so it would not be a surprise to learn that those industries were led by liberals. Furthermore, these were highly competitive grant and loan programs—not usually a hallmark of cronyism. Often less than 10% of applicants were deemed worthy to receive government support.

Nevertheless, a large proportion of the winners were companies with Obama-campaign connections. Indeed, at least ten members of Obama's finance committee and more than a dozen of his campaign bundlers were big winners in getting your money. At the same time, several politicians who supported Obama managed to strike gold by launching alternative energy companies and obtaining grants. How much did they get? According to the Department of Energy's own numbers . . . a lot. In the 1705 government-backed loan program, for example, $16.4 billion of the $20.5 billion in

FRIENDS GIVE FRIENDS BILLIONS OF OUR MONEY

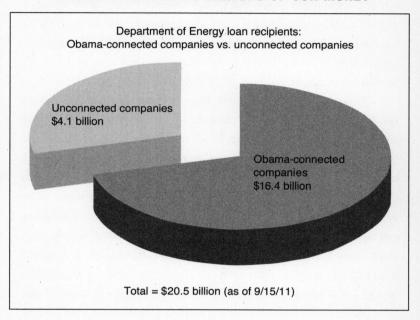

Department of Energy loan recipients:
Obama-connected companies vs. unconnected companies

Unconnected companies
$4.1 billion

Obama-connected
companies
$16.4 billion

Total = $20.5 billion (as of 9/15/11)

loans granted went to companies either run by or primarily owned by Obama financial backers—individuals who were bundlers, members of Obama's National Finance Committee, or large donors to the Democratic Party.[4] The grant and guaranteed loan recipients were early backers of Obama, before he ran for President, people who continued to give to his campaigns and exclusively to the Democratic Party in the years leading up to 2008. Their political largesse is probably the best investment they ever made in alternative energy. It brought them returns many times over.

Those who directed these loan programs were themselves fundraisers for the Obama campaign. One might think that the Department of Energy's Loan Program Office, for example, which has doled out billions in taxpayer-guaranteed loans, is directed by a dedicated scientist or engineer. Or perhaps a civil servant with considerable financial knowledge. Instead, the department's loan and grant programs are run by partisans who were responsible for raising money during the campaign from the same people who later came to seek government loans and grants. Steve Spinner, who served on the Obama campaign's National Finance Committee, and was a bundler himself, was the campaign's "liaison to Silicon Valley." His responsibilities included fundraising, recruiting more bundlers, and managing Obama's relationship with a cadre of very wealthy donors. After the 2008 campaign, Spinner joined the Department of Energy as the "chief strategic operations officer" for the loan programs. A lot of the money he helped hand out went to that same cadre of wealthy Silicon Valley campaign donors. He also sat on the White House Business Council, which is made up of Obama-supporting corporate executives.

Another Obama fundraiser who was positioned to lead the allocation of taxpayer money to Obama contributors was Sanjay Wagle, who served as the managing cochairman of Cleantech and Green Business Leaders for Obama, which raised millions for Obama's campaign. Wagle's day job was as a principal at VantagePoint Venture Partners. After the 2008 election, Wagle joined the Obama administration as a "renewable energy grants adviser" at the Department of Energy. VantagePoint owned firms that would later see federal loan guarantees roll in.

Leading the loan programs at the DOE with Steve Spinner was Jonathan Silver, who would serve as executive director. Silver formerly served in the Clinton administration, first as counselor to the secretary of the interior and later as assistant deputy secretary of the Department of Commerce. He is a strict partisan: when it comes to his own campaign contributions, the recipients have all been Democrats. His wife has served as financial director for the Democratic Leadership Council. His business partner, Tom Wheeler, was an Obama bundler, and his wife was an outreach coordinator for the campaign. According to the DOE, as director of the loan programs "Silver will be responsible for staffing the programs, and leading organization analysis, and negotiation."

Silver managed the loans with advice from his "strategic adviser," Steve Spinner. The grants, on the other hand, originated in the office of Cathy Zoi, who served as the assistant secretary of energy for efficiency and renewable energy. (Wagle was her adviser.) Zoi had previously worked in the Clinton White House as the chief of staff on environmental policy, then as the CEO of former Vice President Al Gore's Alliance for Climate Protection. You may be thinking, "So what? Why would we expect anything less of political appointees?" But the numbers don't lie: the recipients of loans and grants from these programs were Obama cronies. Were the funds doled out based on the merits? You decide.

The Government Accountability Office has been highly critical of the way guaranteed loans and grants were doled out by the Department of Energy, complaining that the process appears "arbitrary" and lacks transparency. In March 2011, for example, the

GAO examined the first eighteen loans that were approved and found that *none* were properly documented. It also noted that officials "did not always record the results of analysis" of these loan applications. A loan program for electric cars, for example, "lacks performance measures." No notes were kept during the review process, so it is difficult to understand how loan decisions were made. The GAO further declared that the Department of Energy "had treated applicants inconsistently in the application review process, favoring some applicants and disadvantaging others." As the GAO noted in another report, the Recovery Act "never defined what was meant by transparency." Similarly, the Department of Energy's inspector general, Gregory Friedman, who was not a political appointee, chastised the alternative energy loan and grant programs for their absence of "sufficient transparency and accountability." He has testified that contracts have been steered to "friends and family."[5]

Friends indeed. The Department of Energy loan and grant programs might be the greatest—and most expensive—example of crony capitalism in American history. Tens of billions of dollars were transferred to firms controlled or owned by fundraisers, bundlers, and political allies, many of whom—surprise!—are raising money for Obama again.

The stated goal of the energy giveaways was to create "green jobs." Yet many of these grants and loan guarantees created few or no jobs, according to the federal government's own records. Often, taxpayer money was given to politically connected companies for projects that were already under way or even completed. Often these companies were money losers that needed government funds to stay in business or turn a profit. By the White House's own admission in internal memos, these grants and guaranteed loans proved to be very lucrative for key political financiers. Several huge checks or loan guarantees were given to small companies with revenues of less than $1 million.

In a memorandum for the President, signed on October 25, 2010, and leaked to the media, senior White House officials Larry Summers, Ron Klain, and Carol Browner explained what an economic boon the grants and loans were to the companies involved. Many of the companies had "relatively small private equity (as low as 10%)," reads the memo, while generating "an estimated return on equity of 30%." Those companies would have been hard-pressed to negotiate that sort of arrangement in the private sector. The memo further points out that if you win government money, it can make all the difference between success and failure. A wind farm can cost 55% less than it would for a company that didn't get government support. Government grants cut costs in half for some solar energy companies. The memo also makes clear that the grant review process was not handled solely by the Department of Energy; the White House staff itself was involved in picking winners and losers. The memo notes that the grants and loans receive a "policy review" by the White House.[6]

White House involvement is particularly interesting because several loans appear to have gone to companies with direct connections to senior White House staff. Granite Reliable Wind, for example, was offered $135 million in loan guarantees. Why is that significant? Because it is largely owned and managed by CCMP Capital, which is where the White House Deputy Chief of Staff Nancy-Ann DeParle had been managing director before joining the Obama administration.

The alternative energy loan and grant programs were originally created in 2005, but they were not very active. Indeed, hardly any loans and grants were offered during the Bush years. The reason? The 2005 law required that the companies receiving loans or grants have a sizable amount of their own money in the game, a "down payment" on projects. But the 2009 stimulus bill removed that provision. Wealthy investors in green-tech companies could now get large government "investments" with very little of their own money at risk.

These government grants and loan guarantees are important not only because they provide access to taxpayer (or taxpayer-guaranteed) capital. Such support also serves as a "seal of approval" from the federal government, opening up access to other private capital. The stock prices of firms rise and fall simply on the news that their applications are under consideration. In May 2011, for example, when it was revealed that First Solar, a sustainable-energy company, was merely "in the running" for government loans and grants, the company's stock rose 5% on the news. *Forbes* even speculated that thanks to the government loans and grants, Americans might well "mint several 10-figure fortunes."[7] As Faysal Sohail, the managing director of the venture firm CMEA Capital, told the *San Francisco Business Journal,* "Getting $25 million from the government does make a difference to investors."[8] The crony-capitalist road to riches was simple: invest in a green-tech company, secure a much larger investment from the federal government, take your company public, and make lots of money. Indeed, as President Obama's Council of Economic Advisers estimated, by July 2010 the government grants and guaranteed loans had stimulated an additional $134 billion of private investment in green-energy firms.[9]

The attorney and lobbyist Steve Farber, a major donor to the Democratic National Committee and cochair of the host committee for the 2008 convention in Denver, which nominated Obama for President, understood exactly how the system worked. He had raised $40 million for the inauguration, and now he could raise some cash for himself.[10] Shortly after the federal government started writing Recovery Act grant checks, Farber boldly placed an ad in the *Wall Street Journal* touting the services and connections of his firm, Brownstein Hyatt Farber Schreck. "Expertise in sustainable energy law is worth nothing without connections," it read. "Learn how we've helped clients obtain funding from the Department of Energy through the American Recovery and Reinvestment Act."

Farber was blunt, but he spoke the truth in a way that only a lobbyist will sometimes do. He was right: when it came to getting access to tens of billions of dollars in taxpayer money, passed around as a stimulus for the economy, connections were the key.

Another Obama fundraiser, Steve Westly, echoed that sentiment. In addition to amassing more than $500,000 for Obama's election in 2008, Westly cochaired California's Obama for President campaign. Westly is a Silicon Valley venture capitalist who also advises high-tech start-ups on financial matters. And like Farber, he has not been subtle about advertising the Obama connection.

"We believe that with the Obama Administration, and other governments . . . committing hundreds of billions of dollars to clean tech, there has never been a better time to launch clean tech companies," reads his company's website. "The Westly Group is *uniquely positioned* to take advantage of this surge of interest and growth."

In addition to regularly attending White House events and state dinners (he was on hand to greet the Chinese premier), Westly also serves on the advisory board of the Department of Energy. Four companies in which Westly had a major financial stake just happened to receive loans, grants, or stimulus money from the Obama Energy Department: Tesla, Recyclebank, Edeniq, and Amirys Biotechnologies. And at least two other companies that later joined his portfolio, Amonix and CalStar Products, received Department of Energy funding.

As a joint investigation of Westly by ABC News and the Center for Public Integrity makes clear, he confidently traded on his connection to Obama, mentioning it in e-mails to Department of Energy officials with whom he was discussing business.[11] But Westly was only one player in a very large drama.

The first guaranteed loan provided by the Obama administration for alternative energy was massive: $573 million for a solar energy company called Solyndra. The company got a low interest rate and the knowledge that if it could not repay what it owed, the government would pick up the tab. In short, a very nice deal. President Obama paid two visits to Solyndra's California factory to tout the grant. As it turned out, 35% of the company was owned by an Oklahoma billionaire named George Kaiser, who was a bundler for the 2008 Obama presidential campaign. (Each Obama bundler raised a minimum of $100,000 for the election.)[12] Nonetheless, since receiving the loan Solyndra has declared bankruptcy, laid off workers, and closed down its first factory.[13] The economic reality is that Solyndra loses money on every solar panel it sells. The company has never been profitable. The plan was simple, and would become a pattern with other companies: secure government money, go public, and get out. As one investor in Solyndra told the *Wall Street Journal:* "There was a perceived halo around the loan. If we get the loan, then we can definitely go public and cash out."[14] Based on the terms of the taxpayer-backed loan, Kaiser and other investors will be paid *before* the government.

That loan set the tone for a whole series of others, as well as for outright grants offered to a large collection of Obama financiers. One of the biggest apparent winners in the sweepstakes for taxpayer dollars was a company called Leucadia Energy. The company gained approval for a number of projects running into the billions of dollars. It received $260 million for an industrial carbon capture project in Lake Charles, Louisiana; approval for $1.6 billion in loan guarantees for a coal gasification project in Indiana; and another $1.6 billion for a synthetic gas project to be based in Chicago. (Some of these projects have faced local opposition because of concerns about pollution, and have not been completed.)[15]

So how on earth did Leucadia Energy manage to attract so much federal money? According to Manta.com, an aggregator of public information about small businesses, Leucadia at the time of the government's decision had one employee and $120,000 in annual revenue. The company is a subsidiary of Leucadia National, whose chairman and CEO is Ian Cumming. Cumming served as a member of President Obama's 2008 National Finance Committee and was on the 2008 Democratic National Convention Committee. Curiously, Ian Cumming wrote three rather large checks to Democratic Party committees just weeks before his funds were approved. He wrote a total of $69,900 in checks in April 2009.

The ostensible purpose of these massive stimulus loans to Leucadia was to create jobs. But according to a government audit, as of December 2010, eighteen months after the loans were made, the Leucadia projects had resulted in a grand total of three jobs.[16]

A total of $2.1 billion was offered to Solar Trust of America to build a solar facility. Both Citigroup Global Partners and Deutsche Bank have a lot of money at stake, $6 billion. The vice chairman of Citigroup Global Partners was, until recently, Louis Susman. And who is Susman? He sat on Obama's National Finance Committee and raised so much for the Obama campaign that he got the nickname "the Vacuum Cleaner." In appreciation, Obama made him ambassador to Great Britain. Deutsche Bank North America's CEO, Seth Waugh, was an Obama campain bundler. The project's partner is Chevron, which heavily favored Obama over McCain in 2008 campain contributions.[17]

A company called Solar Reserve received $737 million in

Department of Energy grant and loan recipients from the Obama campaign's National Finance Committee

Name	Company	Amount (in millions)	State	Amount contributed
Bruce Heyman (Goldman Sachs)	Cogentrix	$90	Colorado	
David Heller (Goldman Sachs)				
Bruce Heyman (Goldman Sachs)	First Solar	$4,700	California	$76,167 $65,600
David Heller (Goldman Sachs)				
Ian Cumming	Leucadia Energy	$260	Louisiana	
Ian Cumming	Leucadia Energy	$1,600	Indiana	
Ian Cumming	Leucadia Energy	$1,600	Illinois	
Frank M. Clark	Peco Energy	$200	Pennsylvania	$75,100 $193,598
John Rogers Jr.				
Daniel Weiss	Powerspan	$100	North Dakota	$20,857 $12,712
Zeb Rice				
Bob Nelson	Sapphire Energy	$135	New Mexico	$13,300
Louis Susman	Solar Trust of America	$2,100	California	
Steve Westly	Tesla, Edeniq, Recyclebank, and Amyris Biotechnologies	$465	California	$500
Bruce Heyman (Goldman Sachs)	U.S. Geothermal	$96.8	Oregon	
David Heller (Goldman Sachs)				
Total		**$11,346.8**		**$457,834**

INVESTING IN POLITICIANS CAN BE HIGHLY PROFITABLE

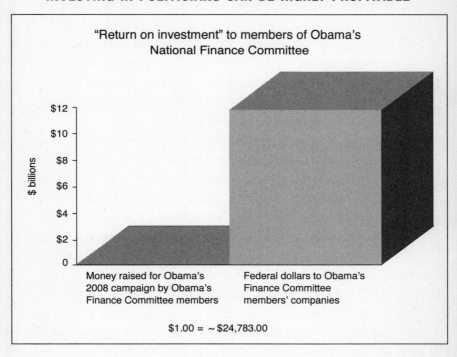

"Return on investment" to members of Obama's National Finance Committee

$ billions

$12
$10
$8
$6
$4
$2
0

Money raised for Obama's 2008 campaign by Obama's Finance Committee members

Federal dollars to Obama's Finance Committee members' companies

$1.00 = ~ $24,783.00

loan guarantees. One of the largest investors in Solar Reserve is CitiAlternatives. The head of CitiAlternatives, before he joined the Obama administration, was Michael Froman. Obama and Froman first met at Harvard Law School, where they served on the *Law Review* together. When Obama ran for the U.S. Senate in 2004, Froman introduced him to major Democratic Party players like Robert Rubin, raised money for the campaign, and advised Obama on policy. When Obama ran for President, Froman helped raise large sums of money on Wall Street. After he secured election, Obama asked Froman to join him in the White House as deputy assistant to the President and deputy national security adviser.

A company called Brightsource received $1.4 billion in loan guarantees to build the Ivanpah Solar Electrical System on federal land in California. Who owns Brightsource? By far the single largest shareholder (25%) is Mr. Wagle's VantagePoint Partners. One of only four partners at the firm is Robert Kennedy Jr., from that famous political family. Although he initially supported Hillary Clinton, Kennedy came around to supporting Obama, comparing him to his father and his uncle. He declared during the election that Obama was a "transformational figure in American history who's been able to excite the same intensity and feeling amoung Americans as I saw during my father's 1968 campaign and my uncle John F. Kennedy's 1960 campaign." Now an environmentalist and an investor in green technologies, Kennedy wrote an article for CNN.com in the summer of 2008 with the apt title "Obama's Energy Plan Would Create a Green Gold Rush." And now Kennedy was in a good position to cash in.

Brightsource badly needed this infusion of taxpayer cash. It had been losing lots of money. It had debt obligations of $1.8 billion and in 2010 lost $71.6 million on revenue of just $13.5 million. The company was blunt in its filings with the Securities and Exchange Commission: "Our future success depends on our ability to construct Ivanpah, our first utility-scale solar thermal power project, in a cost-effective and timely manner." And there were no guarantees: "Our ability to complete Ivanpah and the planning, development and construction of all three phases are subject to significant risk and uncertainty."[18]

A billion dollars in taxpayer money being sent to wealthy investors to bail them out of risky investments—does this sound familiar to anyone?

Another alternative energy company, Abound Solar, cashed in $400 million in grants to increase its production of solar panels. One of the first and largest investors in Abound was billionaire heiress Pat Stryker, who invested through her company, Bohemian. An early financial supporter of the Obama campaign, Stryker has given hundreds of thousands of dollars to Democrats, $87,000 to Obama's Inauguration Committee, and $500,000 to the Coalition for Progress.[19]

A company mentioned earlier, First Solar, received a whopping $4.7 billion in loan guarantees for three solar projects. And who is behind First Solar? The biggest investors include billionaire Ted Turner, a big financial backer of Obama's in 2008, and Goldman Sachs. The financial giant's employees gave Obama more than $1 million in campaign contributions in 2008, making it one of his largest contributors.[20] And two Goldman executives sat on Obama's 2008 National Finance Committee. As a bonus, perhaps, billionaire investor Paul Tudor Jones, another Obama bundler, also owns a stake in First Solar, whose CEO, Michael Ahearn, gives generously (and exclusively) to Democrats.

When news of the loans to First Solar became public, the company's stock jumped more than 6%.[21] For Goldman, it was just one Obama-era payoff. It also raked in another $90 million commitment for a solar site in Colorado, which was being developed by Cogentrix, a wholly owned subsidiary of Goldman Sachs. And U.S. Geothermal, in which Goldman was the second-largest shareholder, was given a $96.8 million guaranteed loan. It was the first geothermal project to complete a loan guarantee from the Department of Energy.[22]

The DOE handed over $102 million in loan guarantees to Record Hill Wind to build a wind farm in Maine. And who heads up Record Hill? Former Governor Angus King, along with Robert Gardiner, the former head of the Maine Public Broadcasting System. Neither has a background in energy. King, however, endorsed Obama in 2008 and campaigned for him.

The other top recipients pulled down various amounts, and in almost every case the numbers and the cronyism were notable. In some instances these projects have been delayed because of local politics, but the federal money has been approved:

- The U.S. Treasury Department gave a $200 million grant to Peco Energy for a smart-grid network—that is, software and equipment designed to help utilities better monitor energy distribution and use. The company is owned by Exelon. Exelon executive Frank M. Clark (who is CEO of the company's ComEd unit) and board member John Rogers Jr. were both members of the Obama campaign's National Finance Committee. White House adviser David Axelrod was a longtime consultant for Exelon. For that $200 million, according to the same federal government audit, Peco (and Exelon) created a total of 102 jobs by December 2010.[23]
- On July 1, 2009, the DOE awarded $100 million to the Basin Electric Power Cooperative in tiny Beulah, North Dakota. The money was for a grant to install "smart meters" to monitor energy consumption. The co-op's partner, which is actually overseeing the work, is Powerspan, a small alterna-

tive energy company whose largest investors include Daniel
Weiss and Zeb Rice of the Angeleno Group. As with Exelon,
both of these executives served on President Obama's National Finance Committee. The other major Powerspan investor is billionaire financier George Soros, who was also an
early Obama supporter. The timing of their investment and
the government grant is interesting. On April 23, 2009, Powerspan revealed that the Angeleno Group and Soros were new
investors. Less than two months later, Department of Energy
Secretary Steve Chu announced the $100 million grant. It
was a big deal for Powerspan, which had raised only half that
amount in private capital up to that point. As of December
2010, a year and a half after Chu's announcement, a government audit revealed that this project had created eight jobs.

- $200 million went to Duke Energy for a smart-grid project. It
  also received $90.4 million for its Notress Windpower proj-
  ect in Texas, for which it had already started construction, in
  May 2008, and which would be finished in April 2009, just
  two months after the stimulus bill became law.[24] That $90
  million was delivered in September 2009, after construction
  was completed.[25] For good measure, the Energy Department
  also granted environmental waivers for both projects.[26] Duke
  Energy CEO Jim Rogers is a major DNC contributor and
  had reportedly been on President Obama's shortlist for energy secretary in December 2008. In March 2011, as reported
  by National Public Radio, Rogers took the "unusual step" of
  committing corporate assets to obtain a $10 million line of
  credit for the National Democratic Convention in 2012.[27]

- A commitment of $308 million was made to Hydrogen En-
  ergy California, LLC, a joint venture between energy giant
  BP and the mining company Rio Tinto. BP appears to be the
  only major oil company that managed to receive substantial

government support. According to the Center for Responsive Politics, BP gave more to Obama's political campaigns than to any other candidate over the past twenty years. In 2008, candidate Obama received $71,000 from the company. The project has created a whopping 23 jobs.[28]

- $115 million in taxpayer money was committed to a company called First Wind, for wind energy projects in Utah and New York. Both projects were already under way when the funds were awarded. The New York project had been started in 2007.[29] The largest equity stakeholder in the company is D. E. Shaw, a hedge fund that is one of the top three contributors to Democrats.[30] The founder of the fund, David Shaw, was an Obama bundler, raising more than $500,000 for the 2008 presidential run. (And like many of the others mentioned here, he is at work on the 2012 election.) D. E. Shaw also employed Larry Summers, who served as the head of President Obama's National Economic Council. Another 42% of First Wind is owned by Madison Dearborn Partners, an investment firm with close ties to then–White House Chief of Staff Rahm Emanuel. The founder of the firm, David Canning, had been a bundler for George W. Bush. But he switched sides in 2008 and gave heavily to Obama. Madison Dearborn gave more to Emanuel's congressional campaigns than did any other business. "They've been not only supporters of mine, they're friends of mine," Emanuel explained on one occasion.[31] In July 2010, First Wind also secured $117 million for a project in Hawaii called Kahuku Wind. It created 125 jobs. The plan was to secure taxpayer money and then go public. But in October 2010 First Wind had to delay its IPO because of weak demand.
- $135 million went to Sapphire Energy for an algae biorefinery, which would create "super algae" that could be con-

verted into energy. ARCH Venture Partners is a major investor in Sapphire. Bob Nelsen, the founding partner, served on
Obama's National Finance Committee during the 2008 campaign. Before 2007, Nelsen considered himself a Republican,
but he switched sides. He was apparently the only Republican
on Obama's finance committee.[32]

- The Treasury Department sent a $60 million stimulus to Van-
  tage Wind Energy, LLC, which is a wholly owned subsidiary of Invenergy, LLC, a Chicago-based company headed by
  CEO Michael Polsky. Polsky is a major Obama donor and a
  financial supporter of the DNC who gave more than $30,000
  to the 2008 Obama campaign and another $50,000 for the
  Obama inauguration. Invenergy also pulled in another $68
  million in taxpayer money for the Beech Ridge Energy Wind
  Farm on September 22, 2010.[33]

- $1.5 billion was approved for Summit Texas Clean Energy,
  LLC. The company is a subsidiary of Summit Energy, located
  on Bainbridge Island, Washington. The company's CEO is
  an attorney named Eric Redman, who is a former staffer for a
  Democratic senator and a major DNC donor. Like the others
  mentioned here, his campaign giving appears to be entirely
  to one party. The project manager for Summit Texas Clean
  Energy is former Dallas Mayor Laura Miller, a Democrat. A
  former newspaper reporter and environmental activist, she
  is perhaps best known as the daughter of the former head of
  Neiman Marcus. She has never worked in the energy industry. As of this writing, Summit had created 8 jobs.

- $465 million in government loans went to Tesla Motors to
  build an electric car. Steve Westly, the venture capitalist, sat
  on the board of Tesla at the time, and his firm owned more
  than 2.5 million shares in the company. (He also personally
  owns an undisclosed number of shares.) Tesla founder Elon

Musk was a major DNC contributor and in 2011 donated
$35,800 to the Obama Victory Fund. (Steve Spinner was an
adviser to Tesla before he joined the Obama campaign.) Tesla
received its taxpayer loan in 2009 and went public in 2010.
The IPO, made possible because of taxpayer money, made the
initial investors even richer: the stock price surged 40%. Steve
Westly made $1.2 million, and Musk $15 million. Since the
IPO, Tesla's stock price has dropped and the company continues to lose money. Tesla's other major investors include Nich-
olas Pritzker, brother of Penny Pritzker, who was the Obama
campaign's finance committee chair, and Sergei Brin and
Larry Page, the founders of Google. The company's CEO at
the time, Eric Schmidt, served as an informal adviser to President Obama. Dan Reicher, director of climate and energy initiatives at Google, was one of the founders of Cleantech and
Green Business Leaders for Obama. When the administration
proposed, in February 2011, to stimulate electric car sales by
offering consumers a $7,500 rebate, stock in Tesla rose 6% on
the news.[34] Google's billionaires were also investors in Brightsource, which won the large loan guarantee mentioned earlier.
$275 million went to Solar City, to install solar panels on mil-
itary bases. Solar City is headed by Elon Musk, and Google is
a large investor.

- The Obama administration also gave $529 million in gov-
ernment-backed loans to Fisker Automotive. Fisker is building a high-end hybrid-electric sports coupe called the Karma,
which will cost $89,000. Fisker's top investors include John
Doerr and former Vice President Al Gore. Fisker continues to
lose money and is heavily in debt.

Tesla and Fisker were in rare company. Only 5 of 130 applicants for the Advanced Technology Vehicles Manufacturing Pro-

gram received funding. (Other recipients in the program were big automakers like Ford and Nissan.) Many of the rejected applicants complained of unfair treatment. In a letter to Secretary of Energy Steve Chu, electric car maker XP Vehicles complained that the company was never contacted by the Department of Energy. "DOE reviewers never even talked to the founder, inventor, engineers, project leads or primary contractors to obtain additional information. Why was staff at DOE during the course of the year positive about the outcome and never asked for additional information?" Other companies that were not politically connected and were shut out—Amp Electric Vehicles was one—expressed similar frustration.[35]

Overall, John Doerr was one of the biggest winners in the taxpayer sweepstakes. A billionaire Silicon Valley venture capitalist, Doerr has donated almost $2 million to Democrats over the past twenty years.[36] His firm, Kleiner Perkins Caufield & Byers (where Al Gore is now a partner), gave more than $1 million to Democrats since 2005. Doerr was an early Obama supporter who opened doors in Silicon Valley and was named as an outside economic adviser and a member of the President's Economic Recovery Advisory Board. As a member of that board he called for increasing fines for carbon pollution and pushing for rules to encourage electric utilities to move to a smart-grid system. As Doerr put it, "God bless the Obama Administration and the U.S. government. We have really got the A-team now working on green innovation in our country." That A-team was busy, of course, rewarding some of Doerr's own investments.

Of the companies listed on Doerr's website as part of his Greentech venture-capital portfolio, well over 50% of them received taxpayer grants or loan guarantees through Obama's stimulus program. Of the 27 listed, at least 16 received direct taxpayer support in the form of loans, grants, or stimulus work: Altarock, Amonix,

Amyris, Aquion Energy, Ausra (which was acquired by Areva), MiaSole, OSIsoft, Primus Power, Transphorm, Recyclebank, Silver Spring, Great Point Energy, Hara, Harvest Power, Lilliputian Systems, and Mascoma. Considering that the acceptance rate in most of the Department of Energy programs was often 10% or less, this is a stunning record. That $2 million Doerr had invested in politics may have provided the best return on investment he had ever seen. Among the results:

- Solar panel maker MiaSole received $102 million in special clean-tech manufacturing credits.
- $24 million went to another Doerr company, Amyris Biotechnologies. The DOE grant was to build a pilot plant to use altered yeast to turn sugar into hydrocarbons. (Steve Westly was also a major shareholder.) Just weeks before the grant was announced, on December 4, 2009, Senator Dianne Feinstein and her husband bought $1 million of equity in the company (November 18). It was their only transaction of the entire year.

With federal money in hand, Amyris went public with an IPO the following year, raising $85 million. John Doerr's firm, Kleiner Perkins, did very well, more than tripling its investment. A $16 million investment was now worth $69 million. It's not clear how Steve Westly or Senator Feinstein did, but it's safe to assume that they did well too. Meanwhile, Amyris continues to lose money, and the grant created forty jobs.[37]

Curiously, in 2011 Senators Tom Coburn and Ben Cardin introduced legislation to immediately repeal the ethanol tax credit. This would threaten biofuel makers such as Amyris. So Senator Feinstein introduced her own bill that would repeal the ethanol tax credit for corn-based ethanol only. That would leave the credit in place for Amyris and actually benefit the company by making competing forms of ethanol more expensive.[38]

- One of the biggest winners for Doerr was Silver Spring Networks, which provides "smart-grid projects." In 2008, Doerr and his partners invested $75 million in the company. Silver Spring doesn't receive grants from the federal government directly; it's a contractor for utilities and other companies that obtained grants to develop a smart grid. Close to 60% of Silver Spring's customers were winners of government grants, totaling more than $560 million.[39]

Silver Spring Networks won a lot of smart-grid projects because of how the stimulus bill was written. It was Al Gore, a partner with John Doerr at Kleiner Perkins, who inspired President-elect Obama not only to invest in clean energy but to put "billions more in the stimulus for construction of the so-called smart grid." Whether Gore revealed to Obama that he had his own money invested in Silver Spring Networks is not known.[40]

Gore was closely wedded to the Obama administration's alternative energy initiative, both directly and indirectly. President Obama asked Gore to serve as his "climate change czar," but the former vice president declined. In his place, Carol Browner, a Gore protégée, got the nod. Rahm Emanuel wondered openly whether Browner would work for Gore or Obama. "When Gore comes and chains himself to the White House gate, it will be Carol's problem," he told colleagues.[41]

The question of Silver Spring's success in the smart-grid business is particularly interesting. The stimulus bill was vague on the protocols and technical standards required. The bill simply read:

(text continues on page 102)

Obama Bundlers, Large Donors, and Supporters

(as of September 15, 2011)

Name	Company	Amount (in millions)
Pat Stryker	Abound Solar	$400
Russ Kanjorski		
Vinod Khosla	AltaRock	$25
John Doerr	Amyris Biotechnologies	$24
Steve Westly		
Michael Polsky	Beech Ridge Energy Wind Farm	$68
Dan Reicher (Google)	Brightsource	$1,400
Larry Page (Google)		
Robert Kennedy Jr.		
Sanjay Wagle		
Sergei Brin (Google)		
Vinod Khosla	Coskata	$250
Jim Rogers	Duke Energy	$200
Paul Tudor Jones	First Solar	$4,700
Ted Turner		
D. E. Shaw	First Wind	$115
David Canning		
Larry Summers		
Al Gore	Fisker Automotive	$529
John Doerr		
Nancy DeParle	Granite Reliable	$135
BP	Hydrogen Energy California LLC	$2,500
Rio Tinto		
David Shaw	Kahuku Wind / First Wind	$117
Vinod Khosla	Nordic Windpower	$16

Name	Company	Amount (in millions)
Jim Rogers	Notress Windpower / Duke Energy	$90.4
Governor Angus King	Record Hill Wind	$102
Dan Reicher (Google)	Solar City	$275
Elon Musk		
Larry Page (Google)		
Sergei Brin (Google)		
Michael Froman	Solar Reserve	$737
Seth Waugh	Solar Trust of America	$2,100
George Kaiser	Solyndra	$573
Jerry Fiddler	Solzyme Inc.	$21.7
John Luongo		
Roger Strauch		
Eric Redman	Summit Texas Clean Energy, LLC	$1,500
Laura Miller		
Dan Reicher (Google)	Tesla Motors	$465
Elon Musk		
Larry Page (Google)		
Nicholas Pritzker		
Sergei Brin (Google)		
Steve Westly		
Michael Polsky	Vantage Wind Energy, LLC	$60
Jonathan Seelig	ZeaChem	$25
Paul Batcheller		
Total		**$16,428.1**

"The Secretary shall require as a condition of receiving funding under this subsection that demonstration projects utilize open protocols and standards if available and appropriate."[41] This language had several Silver Spring competitors crying foul. According to Ed Gray, vice president of regulatory affairs for the smart-meter competitor Elster, the insistence on "open protocols" gave a leg up to Silver Spring at the expense of other providers. Some smart-grid companies rely on other types of standards or use proprietary technology in parts of their smart-grid networks. Silver Spring does not. And Silver Spring seemed not at all defensive about the move. "There's going to be a lot of people complaining," one executive told *USA Today*. "Leadership is helping people adapt to uncomfortable realities."[43]

Billionaire Vinod Khosla was also a big winner in the taxpayer-funded giveaway. Khosla had been the head of Obama's India Policy Team during the 2008 election and contributed to Democratic candidates. He was a major investor in Coskata, a relatively new company whose goal is to make fuel out of waste. Coskata received a $250 million loan guarantee from the federal government.[44] Company executives have been quite clear that one important measure of corporate success is the amount of "government money we attract."[45] Khosla's Nordic Windpower was approved for another $16 million for a wind power manufacturing facility in Idaho. And his company AltaRock secured $25 million in stimulus money.

- In April 2010, $25 million went to ZeaChem, which hired Steve Farber (mentioned above) to lobby on its behalf. One of ZeaChem's major investors are Globespan Capital, where managing director Jonathan Seelig is a Democratic donor (he too has never given to another party). The other major investor is PrairieGold Venture Partners, which is headed by Paul

Batcheller, a former aide to then-Senator Tom Daschle. The grant was awarded to modify a "demonstration sale" biorefinery. According to the federal government, the project created two jobs as of December 2010.

- $21.7 million went to Solazyme, based in South San Francisco. The company was founded and is chaired by Jerry Fiddler, a large Democratic donor (who has also never given to another party). He was a contributor to the Obama Victory Fund, gave $24,000 to the campaign, and made contributions to the DNC. Principal owners of Solazyme include Kennedy's VantagePoint, Lightspeed Ventures, which is headed by John Luongo, another major Obama donor, and the Roda Group, where Roger Strauch is a DNC and Obama campaign supporter. Solazyme had receipts of $38 million in 2010 and lost $13.7 million. Taxpayer money created a total of thirteen jobs. After it received the money, Solazyme announced plans for an IPO.

The list goes on and on. It would take a large team of investigative reporters to untangle every example of cronyism, and it will take more time to assess how many actual jobs these billions of dollars might have helped stimulate. But there is no question that the money failed to produce any significant short-term job gains. The true short-term effect has been to enrich cronies of the party in power. The only thing that many of these grants and loans appear to have in common is how they stimulated the wallets of well-connected investors.

Cathy Zoi, who oversaw the awarding of grants, left the Department of Energy in 2011. Where did she go? She landed as the head of a new green-tech investment fund being established by George Soros, the investor whose firms received taxpayer money through Zoi. As Steve Coll of *The New Yorker* recently wrote, subsidies and support for individual companies amount to "Obama-era crony capitalism," which entails "politically connected invest-ment groups using their inside-information networks to attach themselves to those sections of the federal bureaucracy that will be primed by their party's imperatives of federal spending."[46]

Crony capitalism is good for those on the inside. And it is lousy for everyone else. But it does provide a hybrid-powered vehicle to sustain a large base of rich campaign contributors with taxpayer money.

Imagine for a minute that you are a corporate executive and you start using your company's assets to "invest" in projects that in turn benefit you directly. What would happen? You would be risking possible criminal charges for the misuse of those assets. But if it's taxpayer money? Suddenly it becomes legal. Even acceptable. And for the billionaire who is looking to get a big return on his invest-ment, there are few returns that can be higher than those resulting from campaign contributions. After all, how else can you turn half a million dollars from yourself and your friends into hundreds of millions of dollars after a single election?

Not surprisingly, many of those named here are raising money again, for President Obama's 2012 campaign. As a jobs pro-gram—the stated purpose—these billions in grants and loans were a failure. But as a method for transferring billions in taxpayer funds to friends, cronies, and supporters, they worked perfectly.

6

WARREN BUFFETT:
BAPTIST AND BOOTLEGGER

IN NINETEENTH-CENTURY AMERICA, as part of the "blue law" movement that tried to protect the sanctity and sobriety of the Sabbath, there was a concerted effort to ban alcohol sales on Sunday. It was pushed by what can only be described as an odd alliance: Baptists and bootleggers. Baptists pushed publicly for the ban on moral and religious grounds. And the bootleggers? They pushed for the ban privately, lobbying politicians so they could make bigger profits. Stifling legal alcohol purchases for even one day each week meant added profits for their illegal sales. Bans were enacted state by state, and many blue laws still exist (for example, in Arkansas, Indiana, Minnesota, and Mississippi, among others), although restrictions have been lifted steadily in recent years.

In modern-day Washington, there is a new equivalent to that coalition of Baptists and bootleggers. True believers push a cause that calls for a substantial change in government policy. And opportunists support it because they see a chance for healthy profits.

In these situations, politicians can enrich their friends and allies, and sometimes themselves, while coming off as earnest "Baptists" for a worthy cause. Lobbyists, on the other hand, are widely considered bootleggers, no matter how nobly they cloak their arguments. But what if a capitalist could somehow manage to sound like a Baptist?

Consider Warren Buffett. Often seen as a sort of grandfatherly figure who is above the rough and tumble of politics, Buffett seems to be above the folly and excess of finance too. He lives in Omaha, Nebraska, in a house he first purchased in 1958 for $31,000. He uses folksy words and illustrations to make his point. ("You don't know who's swimming naked," he said during the height of the financial crisis, "until the tide goes out.") He has uttered populist ideas, such as declaring that billionaires don't pay enough in taxes. The title of an article he wrote for the *New York Times* captures the tone: "Stop Coddling Billionaires." And his value-based investing has made himself and his investors at Berkshire Hathaway very rich.

But the image does not always reflect the reality. Warren Buffett is very much a political entrepreneur, whose best investments are often in powerful political relationships, and who in recent years has used taxpayer money as an important vehicle to even greater wealth and profit. Indeed, the success of some of his biggest bets, and the profitability of some of his largest investments, rely on government largesse and "coddling" with taxpayer money.

During the financial crisis in the fall of 2008, Buffett became an important symbol on television. He filled the role of fiscal adult, a responsible father figure in the midst of irresponsible Wall Street speculators. While pushing for calm and advocating specific policies in both public and private, however, he was also investing (sometimes quietly) so he could profit once his policy advice was implemented. This put Buffett in the position of being both the Baptist and the bootlegger, praised for his moral character and at the same time enjoying a trip to the bank.

The crisis started in the summer of 2008, when credit became scarce and Fannie Mae and Freddie Mac and several investment houses teetered on the brink of financial collapse. In the words of the *Guardian*, a London paper, Buffett was "uncharacteristically quiet through much of the financial crisis."[1] It was only on September 23 that he became a highly visible player in the drama, when he invested $5 billion in the investment house of Goldman Sachs, which was overleveraged and short of cash. Buffett gave them a much-needed cash infusion, and made a heck of a deal for himself. Berkshire Hathaway received preferred stock with a 10% dividend yield and an attractive option to buy another $5 billion at $115 a share.[2]

Wall Street was on fire, and Buffett was running toward the flames. But he was doing so with the expectation that the fire department (that is, federal government) was right behind him with buckets of bailout money. As Buffett admitted on CNBC at the time, "If I didn't think the government was going to act, I wouldn't be doing anything this week."

Indeed, Buffett *needed* the bailout. Goldman was not as badly leveraged as some of its competitors, but the crisis was so serious that it was in danger and in need of a government infusion. And beyond Goldman Sachs, Buffett was heavily invested in several other banks that were at risk and in need of federal cash.

He began immediately to campaign for the $700 billion TARP rescue plan that was being hammered together in Washington. The first vote on the funding bill in the House of Representatives failed. But Buffett was in a unique position to help reverse its fate.

Warren Buffett is highly respected in political circles. During the 2008 presidential campaign he was in the unusual spot of being mentioned as a candidate for Treasury secretary by both John McCain and Barack Obama. Buffett made it clear where his loyalties lay: he had been an early financial supporter of Barack Obama's going back to 2004, when Obama had first run for the U.S. Senate and the two men had met. Each had been impressed, and Buffett said at a fundraiser in Nebraska that the two "had a lot of time to talk." In 2008, presidential candidate Obama made it clear that while he got plenty of advice on the campaign trail, "Warren Buffet is one of those people that I listen to." Obama added that he was one of his "economic advisers."[3]

Buffett's role was important too in that several senators and representatives were shareholders in Berkshire Hathaway, and they had to know that passing the bailout bill would bring big returns for their Berkshire stock. Senator Ben Nelson of Nebraska, for example, held between $1 million and $6 million in Berkshire stock, by far his largest asset.[4] Initially resistant to the bailout bill, he ended up voting in favor of it after Buffett bought into Goldman. There were many legitimate reasons to support the bill, and it can hardly be said that Buffet's support was the deciding factor. But his Baptist-bootlegger position was noteworthy for its strength in both directions: a lot of people followed his advice, and he and they made a lot of money by pushing for the bailout.

Throughout the financial crisis and the debate over the stimulus in early 2009, several members of Congress were buying and trading Berkshire stock. Senator Dick Durbin bought Berkshire shares four times in September and October 2008, over a three-week period, up to $130,000 worth. He bought shares during the debate over the bailout, during the vote, and after the vote. Senator Orrin Hatch bought the stock, as did Senator Claire McCaskill, who bought up to half a million dollars' worth just days after the bailout bill was signed. Some also followed Buffett by buying shares in Goldman Sachs after the bailout. Among them were Congressman John Boehner, Senator Jeff Bingaman, and Congressman Vern Buchanan. In other words, the naked self-interest of the lawmakers who shorted the market based on Ben Bernanke's briefings in September 2008 became more twisted in late 2008 and early 2009: Buffet urged passage of the bailout and put his money where his mouth was, and members of Congress listened to him and invested with him.

Early on in the financial crisis, candidate and Senator Barack Obama had been cautious and lukewarm about a possible bailout. But in the days that followed Buffett's multibillion-dollar play for Goldman Sachs, and with a mounting fear of economic collapse, Obama became a powerful champion of the government rescue. As the top Democrat in the country, he had an important vote. The *New York Times* reported that Senator Obama had "intensified" his efforts to "rally support for the $700 billion financial bailout package" after September 28, 2008. The plan was necessary, said Obama, "to safeguard the economy."[5]

Publicly, Buffett struck a posture of political disinterest. "I'm not brave enough to try to influence the Congress," he told the *New York Times*.[6] But his actions directly contradicted his words. Days later, Buffett held a conference call with House Speaker Nancy Pelosi and House Democrats during which he pushed them to pass the bill. We faced "the biggest financial meltdown in American history," he warned wavering Democrats.[7]

The stakes were high for Buffett personally. If the bailout went through, it would be a windfall for Goldman. If it failed, it would be disastrous for Berkshire Hathaway. Buffett also had large investment stakes in Wells Fargo and U.S. Bancorp, banks that were suffering in the crisis.

The first vote failed, as Washington faced enormous heat from voters angry about the prospect of bailing out Wall Street. On the eve of a second TARP vote in the House, Buffett moved toward the fire again when he bought a $3 billion stake in corporate giant General Electric. Again, as with Goldman, he was able to negotiate advantageous terms, receiving a 10% dividend on his shares. He could also buy $3 billion in stock at discounted terms if he wanted.[8] GE was in even worse financial shape than Goldman, thanks to its financial arm, GE Capital. Eventually it would need $140 billion in taxpayer capital to stay afloat.

Buffett is a genius at public relations. He said he had "confidence in Congress to do the right thing." He appeared to be a savior of Goldman Sachs and GE. He gave members of Congress more reason to join by supporting such firms.

With the passage of the Emergency Economic Stabilization Act, the Treasury Department had $700 billion to make available to financial institutions, and with it the unprecedented authority to pick winners and losers. Access to TARP money was not guaranteed. And the terms of the loans were unclear. There was no transparency and no openness to the process. As the economist Robert Kuttner put it, the TARP proceedings were "being done largely behind closed doors, and the design is by, for and in the interest of large banks, hedge funds, and private equity companies. Because there are no explicit criteria, it's very hard to know" if anyone got special treatment. The entire process, he said, "reeks of favoritism and special treatment."[9]

Having the correct political connections was critical, as usual. A study conducted by four researchers at the Massachusetts Institute of Technology documented the power of those connections as a general phenomenon, before the TARP program began. When

Timothy Geithner was announced as President Obama's nominee for Treasury secretary, it "produced a cumulative abnormal return for Geithner-connected financial firms of around 15% from day 0." The stock market reflects the cumulative thinking of all investors, and they assumed Geithner would be able to reward his friends directly or indirectly. Conversely, when there was word that Geithner's nomination might be derailed by tax issues, those same firms were hit hard with "abnormal negative returns." The MIT researchers systematically examined firms that had corporate ties to Geithner, had executives who served with him on other boards, or had other direct relationships. According to the researchers, "The quantitative effect is comparable to standard findings" in Third World countries that had weak institutions and higher levels of corruption.[10] Think of it: our markets react to these government actions the same way they do in a corrupt developing country. Crony capitalism pays, and the market knows it.

Of course Buffett was not the only one connected in Washington. Goldman Sachs also had a direct line to Treasury Secretary Hank Paulson, its former managing partner, as well as incoming officials in the Obama administration. But Buffett was far better liked by the American public than the executives at Goldman Sachs. Politically, he was a far more effective advocate for bailout funds than Paulson could ever be.

Another study, from the University of Michigan School of Business, found that "firms with political connections" were much more likely to get TARP funds than firms that were not well connected. The study looked at how much money firms contributed to election campaigns, through PAC contributions and donations by executives, as well as how much companies spent on lobbyists. Ironically, the study found that those politically connected firms actually underperformed unconnected firms despite the infusion of federal funds. In other words, poorly run, well-connected firms got the loot.[11]

The fact that politically connected banks got good deals from the Treasury was not lost on the banking industry. Robert Wilmers, the chairman and CEO of M&T Bank, said at the time, "The pattern is clear, the bailout money and the perks are concentrated among the big banks, the ones who pay the lobbyists and make the campaign contributions, while the healthy banks pay the freight."[12]

Buffett needed the TARP bailout more than most. In all, Berkshire Hathaway firms received $95 billion in bailout cash from the Troubled Asset Relief Program. Berkshire held stock in Wells Fargo, Bank of America, American Express, and Goldman Sachs, which received not only TARP money but also $130 billion in FDIC backing for their debt. All told, TARP-assisted companies constituted a whopping 30% of his entire publicly disclosed stock portfolio. As one investigation by the *Houston Chronicle* put it, Buffett was "one of the top beneficiaries of the banking bailout."[13]

Buffet demanded better terms for his Goldman investment than the government received for its bailout. His dividend was set at 10%, the government's was set at 5%. Had the bailout not gone through, and had Goldman not been given such generous terms under TARP, things would have been very different for Buffett. As it stood, the arrangement with Goldman earned Berkshire about $500 million a year in dividends. "We love the investment!" he exclaimed later to Berkshire investors. His stake in General Electric was also profitable. As Rolfe Winkler of Reuters bluntly put it, "Were it not for government bailouts, for which Buffett lobbied hard, many of his company's stock holdings would have been wiped out."[14]

By April 2009, share prices for Goldman had more than doubled.[15] By July 2009, it was reported that Buffett had already yielded a return of $2.5 billion for his investment.

Later, astonishingly, Buffett would publicly complain about the bailouts in his annual letter to Berkshire investors, claiming that government subsidies put Berkshire at a *disadvantage*. As he put it, funders "who are using imaginative methods (or lobbying skills) to come under the government's umbrella—have money costs that are minimal," whereas "highly-rated companies, such as Berkshire, are experiencing borrowing costs that . . . are at record levels." Berkshire, of course, is simply a holding company representing a long list of investment assets—including investments in eight banks that were helped by the FDIC's Temporary Liquidity Guarantee Program. As Winkler later put it, "It takes chutzpah to lobby for bailouts, make trades seeking to profit from them, and then complain that those doing so put you at a disadvantage."

One financial observer, Graham Summers of Phoenix Capital Research, claimed that what Buffett did was "a serious conflict of interest AND seriously bordering on insider trading."[16] But what Buffett did was entirely legal. It was an exercise in crony capitalism and manipulation, but he broke no law. He simply used his political connections to secure huge profits with taxpayer money.

There are two questions to ask about this legal behavior. First, how can so many people listen to Warren Buffett's policy advice without considering how self-interested it might be? Second, and more important, how are our politics warped by deep-pocketed, heavily invested advisers?

After the bailout bill passed, Warren Buffett sat down and wrote Treasury Secretary Henry Paulson a four-page private letter proposing a larger solution to the financial crisis that would clean up the toxic assets that were plaguing so many financial institutions. Buffett came up with something he called the public-private partnership fund: a quasi-private fund backed by the U.S. government that would buy bad loans and other rapidly sinking investments. He proposed that for every $10 billion put up by the private sector, the federal government would kick in $40 billion. As Paulson put it in his memoir, "I knew, of course, that as an investor in financial institutions, including Wells Fargo and Goldman Sachs, Warren had a vested interest in the idea."[17]

The bootlegger's interest does not necessarily mean the Baptist's ideas are wrong. The proposal was examined by the Treasury Department, but with Henry Paulson leaving at the end of President Bush's term, it would fall to the incoming secretary, Tim Geithner, to act on it. Geithner tweaked the plan and announced it in March 2009. It was largely seen as a boon to banks, especially to large banks, which had too much bad debt.

But what did Buffett do between the time he first wrote the letter in the fall and Geithner's announcement in March? He bought more bank stocks. According to Berkshire's quarterly reports, Buffett's firm bought 12.4 million shares of Wells Fargo in this period, and another 1.5 million shares in U.S. Bancorp. When Geithner announced the Public-Private Investment Program, bank stocks rallied and Buffet's holdings did very well. We don't know the exact price that Buffett paid for these millions of shares because he is not required to list the dates he bought them in his quarterly reports. But we do know that those banking stocks all jumped after Geithner unveiled his PPIP. Wells Fargo, which was trading at around $20 per share early in 2009, jumped to $30 a share in the weeks following Geithner's announcement. U.S. Bancorp did even better. It had hit a low of $8 a share in February 2009 and jumped to more than $20 a share by May. And of course Buffett already owned tens of millions of shares in a whole host of financial stocks, such as American Express and M&T Bank, which also benefited.

He did very well with Goldman Sachs and GE too, after they received their bailout money. His net from General Electric as of April 2011 was $1.2 billion. His profits from the Goldman deal by then had exceeded the gains of July 2009, reaching as high as $3.7 billion. He was betting on his ability to help secure the bailout. The bet was a good one.[18]

In the fall of 2010, Buffet wrote "Thank You, Uncle Sam," an op-ed in the *New York Times* in which he praised the role that government played in stabilizing the markets throughout the crisis.[19] There was no disclaimer or disclosure of how much he personally benefited from the TARP or the Public-Private Investment Program. He simply praised it as good public policy. At the bottom of the article he was identified in a short biography: "Warren E. Buffett is the chief executive of Berkshire Hathaway, a diversified holding company."

With tongue sarcastically in cheek, journalist Ira Stoll, the former managing editor of the *New York Sun*, suggested the bio might have been more accurate with a bit of rewriting: "Warren Buffett, the largest crony capitalist in the world, shareholder of GE, Goldman Sachs, Wells Fargo, US Bancorp, M&T Bank, and American Express, as well as competitor of private equity and hedge fund firms that have been threatened with new taxes and regulations, and behind the scenes, insider adviser to most of the government officials mentioned above."[20]

Again, to be clear, even though Buffet was the one who proposed the public-private partnership, there is absolutely nothing illegal about lobbying for a policy while investing in the potential winners if that policy is adopted. But consider this: had Buffet been pushing a private investment house to make an acquisition that would benefit certain stocks while quietly buying shares in those same stocks, he would possibly have been investigated for insider trading. Indeed, this is what his lieutenant David Sokol was accused of doing, landing him in legal hot water. Sokol apparently bought shares in Lubrizol, a chemical company, and then encouraged his employer, Berkshire Hathaway, to buy a large stake in the company, thereby driving up the price of the stock.[21] All Buffett did differently was use the federal government instead of a private company to boost the prices of certain stocks. This, of course, is why crony capitalism is so attractive to financiers. First, it's legal. Moreover, it is often more remunerative than the illegal private-sector version might be. Because government officials are dealing with other people's money, they are less likely to drive a hard bargain than a private firm would.

Buffett has long been a believer that corporate-government partnerships are investment opportunities. While Buffett is famous for owning Dairy Queen and other all-American private companies, two of his largest holdings are in railroads and regulated utilities. He regularly lobbies for and counts on significant public money to make them more profitable.

After the financial crisis in the fall of 2008 appeared to be easing, Buffett turned his attention to championing the stimulus program for the Obama administration. When he went on television to proclaim his support for a stimulus, he was never asked what he might get out of the deal. A candid answer would have taken up many valuable minutes of airtime.

In late 2009, Buffett made his largest investment ever when he decided to buy Burlington Northern Santa Fe Railway (BNSF). It was not just a bet on the financials of the railroad industry; it was also a huge bet on his friend President Obama's budget priorities. As the *Wall Street Journal* reported, "Berkshire Hathaway Inc.'s planned purchase of Burlington Northern Santa Fe Corp. represents a bet that upcoming Washington policies to improve infrastructure and combat climate change will be a boon to the freight-railroad industry. President Barack Obama has said railroad investment will be a cornerstone of his transportation policies, given the environmental benefits and improved mobility that come with taking cars and trucks off roads."[22]

Others in the railroad industry saw Buffett's involvement as very helpful, precisely because he was so politically connected. "It's a positive for the rail industry because of Buffett's influence in Washington," explained Henry Lampe, president of the Chicago South Shore & South Bend, a short-haul railroad.[23]

Buffett bought the BNSF just as the Obama administration was beginning a series of initiatives to rapidly expand the government's commitment to spending on railroads.[24] After Buffett took over the company, he dramatically increased spending on lobbyists. Berkshire spent $1.2 million on lobbyists in 2008, but by 2009 its budget jumped to $9.8 million, where it has generally remained. Pouring money into lobbying is perhaps the best investment that Buffett could make.[25]

President Obama's plans to invest heavily in railroads, including a commitment to high-speed rail, position BNSF to benefit handsomely. In the Seattle area there have already been discussions between local officials and BNSF about either leasing or selling its rail lines for an intercity project. And that's just the start. A map of the BNSF lines around the country overlaps nicely with the government's proposed high-speed rail lines, from Seattle to Florida, California to the Northeast. Buffett is geographically and strategically positioned to profit from those government-funded rail systems, should they be built.

All together, in the stimulus package created in 2009, the federal government set aside $48 billion (of the total $787 billion) for infrastructure improvement, some of which goes to railroads. How much will BNSF benefit? It's nearly impossible to calculate. Type BNSF on the Recovery.gov website, which tracks grants, subsidized loans, and contracts signed under the stimulus, and you find

1,800 entries, including everything from $36 million grants from the Department of Homeland Security to money from the Environmental Protection Agency.

Buffett also owns MidAmerican Energy Holdings, which received $93.4 million in stimulus money. General Electric, of which he owns a $5 billion stake, was one of the largest recipients of stimulus money in the country.

As Buffett often does, he puts his ideas in down-home terms in his famous annual letter to Berkshire investors. He doesn't mention lobbyists, government funds, bailouts, or stimulus grants. "We see a 'social compact' existing between the public and our railroad business, just as it is the case with our utilities," he said in his 2010 annual letter to shareholders. "If either side shirks its obligations, both sides will inevitably suffer. Therefore, both parties to the compact should—and we believe will—understand the benefit of behaving in a way that encourages good behavior by the other. It is inconceivable that our country will realize anything close to its full economic potential without it possessing first-class electricity and railroad systems." He further noted that both businesses "require wise regulators who will provide certainty about allowable returns so that we can confidently make the huge investments required to maintain, replace, and expand the plant."

The term "social compact" sounds benign. But when did American voters make a compact to turn one of the richest men in America into one of the biggest recipients of taxpayer subsidies?

In August 2011, Buffett vacationed with President Obama on Martha's Vineyard and they discussed the economy. Shortly after that, he agreed to host an Obama reelection fundraiser in New York City, for which contributors could buy VIP tickets for $35,800 to meet Buffett and talk about the economy.[26]

It has long been known to be Warren Buffett's style to base major financial decisions on a few phone calls. As fellow investor Steven Rattner pointed out, "Warren Buffett has shown that superb investing need not entail the months of due diligence and deliberation that private equity firms typically apply to a deal. Buffett has been known to make successful multibillion-dollar bets on the basis of a few meetings or phone calls."[27] That is particularly true if those phone calls are going to Washington.

Warren Buffett is a financial genius. But even more important for his portfolio, he's a political genius.

7

CRONIES ON PARADE: HEDGE FUNDS, DEFENSE CONTRACTORS, COLLEGES, BIG OIL . . . AND GEORGE SOROS

MOST CAPITALIST CRONIES are neither Baptists nor bootleggers. They do nothing illegal, but neither do they claim to be holy. Instead, they quietly lobby Congress, and their fortunes rise and fall on policy decisions rather than market competition. In this chapter, we will consider a wide range of examples, from finance to manufacturing to education.

Perhaps the best investment a hedge fund can make these days is not in a financial wizard but a politician. Hedge funds and financiers are becoming more political than ever before. And political figures and government appointees with no background in finance (former Vice Presidents Dan Quayle and Al Gore, and former Secretary of State Madeleine Albright, for example) have launched their own investment funds. "The former politician/investment guru fraternity appears to be growing," noted one industry observer.[1] And former politicians are finding a career that can be even more lucrative than lobbying: providing "political intelligence" to investment funds, based on private conversations with congressional staffers and sitting senators.

In the world of investment finance it is increasingly important to be well connected politically. As briefly mentioned earlier, one study by two economists looked at 351 hedge funds between the years 1999 and 2008 and found that "politically connected" hedge funds—that is, funds that hired lobbyists and made campaign contributions—had a much better rate of return on investments than those which were not. Political connections created "an abnormal rate of return of 1.4 to 1.6 percent per month." The study explained that "connected funds possess an informational advantage in trading politically sensitive stocks." The study also found that when a given hedge fund switched from being apolitical to getting into the political game, its performance increased by an impressive average of 2% to 2.9% per month. The economists also discovered that the more hedge funds gave to political candidates and the more they hired lobbyists, the more they tended to invest in politically sensitive stocks that were influenced by government actions.[2] As the authors put it, "Connected fund managers exhibit a bias towards politically sensitive stocks (both in terms of trading and holdings) and they outperform significantly in these political stocks."[3]

It is commonsensical. The simple fact is that politically connected hedge fund managers and billionaire financiers can make a lot of money based on information gleaned from politicians and government officials. And it is not illegal for a politician to share this information. If an official gets paid directly for it, however, he risks a bribery charge. Former Congressman Brian Baird warned that the financial stakes are so high, "the possibility of direct kickbacks [is] enormous."[4] So the payback must be subtle.

Elliott Portnoy, a lobbyist in Washington, says that the biggest field of growth for lobbyists is not in influencing legislation but in obtaining "political intelligence" for hedge funds and large investors. "There are a lot of savvy investors who have realized that there is a lot of money to be made from what Congress does," Portnoy said.[5] One congressional staffer was even more blunt when he told the *Wall Street Journal*, "The amount of insider trading going on in these halls is incredible."[6]

How does this process happen? Consider a 2008 farm bill analyzed by the *Wall Street Journal*. Money managers and hedge funds paid lobbyists big money to track the bill, because the stakes were enormous for ethanol producers, timber companies, and farm equipment manufacturers. "I get a lot of people asking about legislation who appear to be monitoring it rather than lobbying it," a Senate tax staffer commented to the *Journal* about the bill.[7] The hedge fund investors can make money no matter how Congress votes—if they receive advance warning.

Access to government information is critical. And being on good terms with the gatekeepers of that information—elected officials, political appointees, and bureaucrats—can make all the difference between getting rich and getting hammered in the market. Consider, for example, the recent interaction between political appointees at the Pentagon and investment advisers that track defense-related stocks. As the *New York Times* reported in February 2011, senior Pentagon officials began meeting in secret with investment advisers in New York to give them information regarding defense-related companies. The message was direct: even with defense cutbacks on the horizon, "the Pentagon is going to make sure the military industry remains profitable." As those officials made clear, the Pentagon was opposed to mergers among large defense companies, but it would encourage mergers among smaller contractors.

This kind of information is critically important to investors. The Pentagon is basically the sole customer of most of these defense companies. What the military says and does will determine who thrives and who dies.

Deputy Defense Secretary William J. Lynn held a private meeting with about a dozen Wall Street analysts in October 2010 and laid out the Pentagon's cost-cutting plans "in astonishing detail," reported the *Times*. The analysts at the meeting were sworn to secrecy; nonetheless, the meeting had a noticeable effect on the market. The Big Five defense contractors—Lockheed Martin, General Dynamics, Raytheon, Northrop Grumman, and Boeing—all saw their stocks rise shortly after that October meeting.

Who was invited to the meeting? Who was excluded? We may never know.[8]

Early in 2011, a liberal organization called Citizens for Responsibility and Ethics in Washington (CREW) released some alarming material concerning the possible market manipulation of stocks involving Steven Eisman, a well-known short seller. Eisman was featured in Michael Lewis's book *The Big Short* for making huge profits by betting against the subprime mortgage market just before the 2008 financial meltdown.

The research by CREW caught the attention of Republican Senator Tom Coburn, who called for an investigation. According to documents unearthed by CREW, Eisman was advising the Department of Education, discussing problems associated with for-profit colleges. At a meeting with senior officials on April 26, 2010, he went so far as to compare the schools to subprime mortgage lenders. Two days later, one of the officials at the meeting, Deputy Undersecretary Robert Shireman, delivered a speech in St. Paul, Minnesota, in which he drew the same comparison. After his speech, the share prices of for-profit education companies Career Education and the Apollo Group dropped 12% and 6%, respectively. On May 26, Eisman himself delivered a speech titled "Subprime Goes to College," again making the comparison. After the speech the share prices of the for-profit companies ITT Education Services and Corinthian Colleges each declined 3%. In June, Eisman testified before Congress and delivered the same message.

All of this coincided with government action that called for tough new regulations of for-profit colleges. Of course, there is nothing wrong with officials at the Department of Education getting briefings and making speeches. But why would the department listen to a short-selling investor who is no expert on education? Eisman has refused requests to reveal whether he was shorting for-profit college stocks during this period, but given that that is his day job, members of Congress on both sides of the aisle have called for an investigation.[9]

Or consider the suspicious trading activity around the Obama administration's decision to tap the Strategic Petroleum Reserve (SPR) during the summer of 2011. CNBC looked at trades made shortly before the release of some of the nation's stockpiled oil and discovered that there was a curious spike in trading. Dennis Gartman, a hedge fund manager who also publishes the *Gartman Letter*, constructed a timeline of the trade activity and concluded: "When presented this information in this simple but elegant format, how can we not believe that someone in a position of some authority did indeed know what was in the works regarding the SPR?" His comments were echoed by Ross Clark, an investment adviser at CIBC Wood Gundy: "Call me a cynic, but there appears to have definitely been money made on inside information. As a rule of thumb, some of the best opportunities occur by trading opposite the headline news once prices stabilize."[10]

Human nature being human nature, such actions are not unique to the Obama administration. Traders, speculators, and investors seek out friends in both political parties. And politicians, political appointees, and bureaucrats see the value in helping out wealthy friends and contributors in the hope that the favor will be returned when they need it. But what has changed in recent years is the amount of money involved, and the power of the federal government to move markets and make people very rich.

The economic stimulus bill passed in 2009 provided a much greater opportunity to make money. The amount of federal expenditures on the table, and the small details embedded in the bill, promised to have an enormous influence on the profitability of hundreds of companies. If you could predict which ones would land large stimulus contracts or which ones would benefit from an arcane sentence in the bill, you would reap impressive investment returns. The legislative and executive actions set off a feeding frenzy among investors with political connections.

One investor who worked hard to profit from the stimulus is the legendary George Soros. Whether he is a Baptist or a bootlegger in this story is hard to say. In a way, it is possible that he is both: a true believer and a profiteer from government policies he has championed. Again, there is nothing illegal about taking on both roles. But as a review of the many ways in which he made smart stimulus bets reveals, the lesson is clear: if you are a big investor, you are a sucker if you don't play the Washington game. The symbiosis of politics and markets has become so blatant, the two realms have become so intertwined, that Washington is essentially putting its thumb on the scale of a massive portion of the American economy—and elite insiders are the ones who benefit most.

George Soros is perhaps the most visible investor in the world after Warren Buffet. He is as famous for his currency trades as for his outspoken political views. And in a world where government actions and policies have such a huge effect on the world of finance, the two spheres are not so separate as one might think.

Soros's spokesman Michael Vachon told a *New Yorker* reporter that "none of his contributions are in the service of his own eco-

nomic interests."[11] Others, such as former *New York Times* colum-
nist Frank Rich, who shares some of Soros's political views, as-
sert that Soros gives "selflessly" to causes.[12] Surely his charitable
donations are motivated by his ideals. He is a significant philanthropic investor in science and education projects around the
world, among other worthy causes. But Soros also makes huge investments whose fate is tied to his political activism.

Soros made his money early on in currency speculation, which
often amounts to a financial bet either for or against a government
policy. For example, in 1992 Soros bet (correctly) against the British pound and famously made $1 billion in a single day. Former
U.S. Chamber of Commerce chief economist Richard Rahn believes that Soros had hints that his bet would succeed. According
to Rahn, he was told by a member of Parliament who was a close
adviser of the chancellor of the exchequer at the time that Soros
was acting on insider information obtained from the French central bank and the German Bundesbank.[13] These banks had previously agreed to support the pound, but when Soros made his
big bet that the pound would have to be devalued, neither European bank joined the Bank of England's fight to maintain its value.
Whether Soros really knew that they would stand aside is entirely
unproven—Rahn's vaguely sourced charge could be wrong. Yet
the value of that policy information would have been extraordinarily high. And investors will sometimes do anything they can to
attach themselves to politicians who can tip them off to information like that.

Soros has long recognized the important intersection between
politics and finance. Mark Malloch Brown, former deputy chief to
UN Secretary-General Kofi Annan, left the United Nations at the
end of 2006. A few months later, he was named vice president of
the Quantum Fund, which is run by Soros. Brown had no experi-

ence in hedge funds, though he had worked with Soros on philanthropic efforts in eastern Europe.[14] His chief value lay in his political connections.

In the United States, Soros has given generously to prominent members of the political class. Since Harry Reid became the Senate minority leader in 2005 and majority leader in 2007, Soros has poured more than $220,000 into the Democratic Senatorial Campaign Committee through a variety of ventures and family members. He was also an early backer of Barack Obama. He donated more than $60,000 to Obama's 2004 Senate run and was vital in building the 2008 Obama campaign's war chest.

As one writer put it, Soros was one of Obama's "first big catches, and within just two months Obama had a New York money machine that rivaled Clinton's." Indeed, many of Obama's earliest campaign financiers came from the hedge fund industry, including Orin Kramer and Brian Mathis. By the first quarter of 2008, Obama had raised more money on Wall Street than either New Yorker in the race—Hillary Clinton or Rudy Giuliani. Goldman Sachs alone kicked in $571,330.[15]

Soros is, of course, free to contribute to any candidate he likes, and to help organize fundraising for them. Other financiers do these kinds of things all the time. What is remarkable is that once Obama was elected, Soros not only provided advice and direction on the President's plans for an economic stimulus, but he also had regular private consultations and meetings with White House senior advisers while he was making investment decisions related to the stimulus program. Section 13(f) of the Securities Exchange Act of 1934 requires "institutional investment managers" to report certain positions in publicly traded securities by filing a Form 13 on a quarterly basis. However, these managers are not required to report transactions or prices. Thus it is extremely difficult to determine how profitable (or not) investments by an investment manager like Soros have been. What is certain is that Soros seemed to have a keen ability to anticipate what Washington was going to do and position himself to potentially profit handsomely from it.

Days after President Obama was elected, Soros was helping to set the agenda. Soros had regular meetings with senior White House officials. He met with Obama's top economist, Larry Summers, on February 25, 2009. He also had meetings in the Old Executive Office Building with senior officials on March 24 and 25 as the stimulus was being forged.[16] He was later involved in private discussions concerning widespread financial reform.[17]

Soros was also a financial backer of the Center for American Progress, which functioned as Obama's think tank. John Podesta, who headed CAP, was Obama's transition director. Several CAP policy ideas became part of Obama's agenda. Soros said at the time, "I think we need a large stimulus package, which will provide funds for state and local government to maintain their budgets, because they are not allowed by the constitution to run a deficit. For such a program to be successful, the federal government would need to provide hundreds of billions of dollars. In addition, another infrastructure program is necessary. In total, the cost would be in the 300 to 600 billion dollar range."[18] On another occasion he advocated for a "well-advanced fiscal stimulus package" to help the American economy.[19] In these general terms, he spoke like a Baptist.

But as tens of billions of federal dollars became available, he invested like a bootlegger. In the first quarter of 2009, Soros nearly doubled his holdings in Hologic, a manufacturer of diagnostic equipment, which benefited from federal spending on medical systems. He more than tripled his holdings in Emulex, a leading designer of fiber channels and software products and a government contractor that would win big with infrastructure spending. He also tripled his holdings in EMC, a data storage company, which claimed on its website that "EMC's products and services can support stimulus programs tied to creating and preserving jobs in transportation, education, healthcare, carbon-emission reduction, and more."[20] He also increased his holdings in Teradata by almost 60%. Teradata provides computer and network technologies to the federal government, including the military and Medicare and Medicaid.[21]

He also bought 210,000 shares in Cisco Systems, another big stimulus winner, and shares in Vulcan Materials, which is the nation's foremost producer of construction materials such as concrete. The company stood to do big business because of infrastructure spending.

One of Obama's stimulus initiatives was for updating Internet networks around the country. Soros bought shares in Extreme Networks in the first quarter of 2009. Months later, the Internet company was "pushing broadband networks into rural America, as part of President Obama's broadband strategy."[22] He also increased his holdings in Radware, an Internet technology company, by 476%. Radware provides high-tech services and computer applications to twelve government agencies.[23]

In the second quarter of 2009, Soros bought shares in Blackboard, a sizable stimulus recipient of technology grants in education. He also snapped up shares in Burlington Northern Santa Fe and CSX, which would benefit from President Obama's stimulus plans for railroad transportation. Later he bought shares in Cognizant Technology Solutions, an information technology company that was an important health care vendor as well as an education technology provider. Cognizant was a two-fer, a winner in both realms. Indeed, the company reported in one of its publications that business was strong "due to federal economic stimulus funds."[24]

President Obama's stimulus for alternative energy companies and for developing a smart grid for utilities was also an area where Soros traded aggressively. He snapped up Constellation Energy Group stock (300,000 shares), which received $200 million in federal stimulus money through a natural gas utility subsidiary. He also bought a stake in Covanta (4.6 million shares), a clean-energy company and federal grant recipient. Covanta also received money through earmarks from members of Congress.

Again, to be clear, it is not necessarily the case that Soros had specific insider tips about any government grants. You might argue that any smart investor would have guessed that economic stimulus funds would be used to promote infrastructure improvements, green energy, and certain high-tech ventures. Yet the list of specific investment decisions by Soros is closely aligned with the list of grant recipients. In addition to the examples above:

- In the first quarter of 2009, Soros made an initial purchase of more than 1.5 million shares in American Electric Power, a utility that had invested heavily in an energy project called FutureGen. FutureGen was a government-backed zero-emissions electric power project launched by the Bush administration in 2003, which at first focused on a coal-fueled electric plant in Illinois, but had been subsequently canceled before the 2008 election. President Obama revived the project in June 2009 and poured $1 billion of taxpayer money into it. Soros bought his shares just in time for the revival.[25] Months later, the company received another grant, this one for a coal plant in West Virginia.
- Soros scooped up shares in Ameren, a Midwest utility com-

pany that was given a $540 million clean-energy grant from the Department of Energy in conjunction with NextGen.

- Soros for the first time bought shares in Entergy, an energy utility company, to the tune of almost one million shares. Entergy would go on to get numerous grants from the Department of Energy, for smart grids, smart meters, and other federal stimulus programs.

- He also bought NRG Energy, more than half a million shares' worth. The company owns power-generating facilities and was a recipient of Department of Energy grants, including one for $154 million, announced by Energy Secretary Steven Chu.[26]

- Soros bought a quarter of a million shares of Public Service Enterprise Group, another recipient of Department of Energy federal stimulus grants.[27]

- Soros held a stake in Allegheny Energy (250,000 shares) and PPL (175,000 shares), which also won lucrative grants from the Department of Energy. He bought shares in Edison International, yet another utility company that cashed in on DOE grants.

- Soros also invested in a small ethanol-producing company called BioFuel Energy, which had created a new gasoline containing 15% ethanol. At the time, the EPA had approved a limit of 10% ethanol in gasoline. BioFuel Energy owns and operates two of the largest dry-mill ethanol production facilities in the United States. Getting approval for an increase in the limit, to 15%, would obviously benefit the company. As the EPA debated the idea, stock in the company jumped from about $1.50 to $2.94 a share. The EPA eventually approved the mandate.

- Soros invested in Powerspan, a clean-energy technology company, in April 2009. His timing was perfect. Weeks later, on July 1, Powerspan was awarded a $100 million grant from the Department of Energy for smart-grid work.

How did these investments perform for Soros? It is very difficult to tell. He is not required to disclose the price he paid or the price at which he sold his shares. We don't know the dates of the transactions, only that they occurred during a particular three-month period. What we do know is that his investment decisions aligned remarkably closely with government grants and transfers. It would appear that one of the world's smartest investors chose a strategy based on political decisions—whether he knew about the decisions in advance or just guessed extremely well.

Soros undoubtedly viewed this the way that General Electric CEO Jeffrey Immelt did when he predicted in early 2009, "The global economy, and capitalism, will be 'reset' in several important ways. The interaction between government and business will change forever. In a reset economy, the government will be a regulator; and also an industry policy champion, a financier, and a key partner."[28]

Soros recognizes and understands that good politics can lead to good profits as the government plays an increasingly central role in the economy. When he decided recently to launch a new green-tech fund, called Silver Lake Kraftwerk, to invest over $1 billion, Soros selected as its chief none other than Cathy Zoi, the former assistant secretary of energy efficiency and renewable energy. Political access has become the key to financial success.

America's financiers have learned their lesson: profits are better in Washington, among insiders, than on the open market. Far from being the purveyors of pure free market capitalism, as we imagine, they are all too often riding in the wake of government money. Wouldn't it be better if they focused exclusively on financial and business matters? Crony capitalism favors the politically active, and the manipulative. It does not favor one party over the other. It does not care about policy. It just knows how to make money off any policy—your tax dollars, leveraged to the rich.

Part Three

BREAKING THE BACK OF
CRONY CAPITALISM

8

SOME ARE MORE EQUAL THAN OTHERS

If this spirit is ever corrupted to the point that it will tolerate a law which does not apply to both the legislature and the people, then the people will be prepared to tolerate anything but liberty.

— *FEDERALIST* NO. 57

Nearly all men can stand adversity, but if you want to test a man's character, give him power.

— ABRAHAM LINCOLN[1]

THERE IS SOMETHING inherently wrong with a professional athlete gambling on his own game. It's unethical because he can influence the outcome of the game and profit from his manipulation. Such gambling is banned in every major sport since it threatens the integrity of the game and runs against our sense of justice.

Very few of us are professional athletes—I have enough problems on the treadmill—but all of us are governed by laws, codes, and rules concerning conflicts of interest.

In the financial world these regulations are everywhere. If you are an investment adviser, for example, you are required to disclose not just actual conflicts of interest, but also potential conflicts of interest. It you own stock in a company and you recommend that stock to others, you had better tell them that you stand to gain if they take your advice. Failure to do so can land you in a lot of legal trouble. If you are a bank regulator, you are not allowed to conduct so much as a simple bank examination if you happen to own any stock in that particular bank.

If you are a federal judge, the law requires that you recuse yourself from cases involving any company in which you own more than $30 worth of stock. If you don't, it's a felony.

On the U.S. Supreme Court, justices recuse themselves all the time for this very reason. Sometimes there is no direct conflict, yet propriety causes members of the court to be extra-careful. In May 2008, for example, four justices recused themselves from considering a case that involved compensation on behalf of citizens of South Africa from more than fifty American companies that were doing business in the country. Apparently the justices believed even the appearance of a remote link with any of the companies might raise concerns. When a case involving Disney World was brought for review before the Supreme Court in March 2008, Justice Samuel Alito recused himself because he owned Disney stock.[2]

The ancient Roman symbol of justice, the goddess Justitia, was often portrayed carrying scales and a sword and wearing a blindfold. These objects are meant to symbolize fairness, justice, and impartiality.

The executive branch of the federal government follows similar ethics rules and laws. If you work for a government agency like the Federal Communications Commission "you may not have a financial interest in any company engaged in the business of radio or wire communication."[3]

Don't even consider actively trading stocks based on executive-branch knowledge. The Securities and Exchange Commission recently launched investigations into two of its own employees who may have traded stock based on inside information. One of the employees, an SEC attorney, sold all of her shares in a large health care company two months before an investigation of that firm was opened. She also sold all her shares in an oil company two days before a colleague began an inquiry into that firm. Another attorney allegedly "traded in the stock of a large financial services company" while the SEC had an ongoing investigation into the firm.[4]

Conflict-of-interest laws are not limited to the federal government. School superintendents across the country are expected to make financial decisions that are to the benefit of their districts—not themselves. If they fail to do so, they can be charged with violating state laws. This applies even if they receive only an indirect financial benefit from their actions. Award a school contract to a relative's company and you will get in trouble.[5]

Even nonprofit organizations are required by the IRS to comply with conflict-of-interest laws. Failure to do so is a punishable offense. And certainly in the private, for-profit sector every large corporation has rules on conflicts of interest. If you use corporate resources for your personal benefit it is generally considered fraud, and you may find yourself in legal trouble. If you don't believe me, just ask former Tyco CEO Dennis Kozlowski. He was convicted in 2005 of accepting millions of dollars in unauthorized bonuses, among other improprieties, and he is serving a jail sentence as a result.

If you work for a major accounting firm, you are asked not to own stock in the companies you are auditing. An accountant must swear a professional oath to "hold himself or herself free from any influence, interest, or relationship in respect to his or her client's affairs, which impairs his or her professional judgment or objectivity."[6]

Corporate executives and officers are expected to reveal conflicts of interest and recuse themselves from decisionmaking that might personally benefit them. They are required by law to report to the SEC any transactions involving corporate stock within forty-eight hours of the transaction.

Many companies have codes of conduct for all employees that prohibit owning shares in a competing firm or supplier, or working for a competing firm or supplier. The conflict of interest is obvious.

If you work for a reputable news organization, chances are that conflict-of-interest rules quite clearly guide your portfolio. The *New York Times* has a strict policy on stock ownership. "No staff member may own stock or have any other financial interest, including a board membership, in a company, enterprise or industry about which she or he regularly furnishes, prepares or supervises coverage. This restriction extends beyond the business beat. A book editor may not invest in a publishing house, a health writer in a pharmaceutical company or a Pentagon reporter in a mutual fund specializing in defense stocks." The fear is, of course, that reporters might slant their reporting because of their personal investments.[7]

These kinds of corporate policies are developed to comply with federal and state laws. The Securities and Exchange Commission has actually gone after reporters who trade on their knowledge for personal gain. In the 1980s, *Wall Street Journal* reporter Foster Winans was the subject of a probe for taking money in exchange for stock tips. He was passing information in not-yet-published col-

umns to a broker who traded on the information. Winans reportedly made less than $30,000 on the scheme. Nonetheless, the SEC
said the reporter "violated [the law] by reason of his failure to disclose to readers of his column his financial interest in the securities about which he wrote and his intent to profit from the rise or
fall of the market in such securities following the publication of the
column in the [*Wall Street*] *Journal*." Winans spent eight months in
jail.[8]

There has been a proliferation of ethics rules in the decades
since Watergate, beginning with the Ethics in Government Act
of 1978. At the same time, Congress, the SEC, and the Supreme
Court have strengthened insider trading laws. So it is perplexing
that, despite all the ink spilled to address ethics in government and
insider trading, members of Congress and their staffs have floated
above the fray. Politicians understand both the specific issue of insider trading and the larger issue of conflict of interest—when it
suits their purposes. When U.S. District Judge Martin Feldman
ruled to overturn the Obama administration's six-month morato-
rium on deep-water drilling in the Gulf of Mexico, six senators
asked for an investigation. Judge Feldman owned stock in Exxon
at the time.[9] In another instance, senators went after medical researchers who were given government grants for pharmaceutical
research while also receiving research money from drug companies. The senators questioned the ability of the researchers to be
impartial. Of course, these senators said nothing about their colleagues (or themselves) trading these very same stocks while writing energy or health care policy.[10]

When it comes to lawmakers applying the conflict-of-interest
standard to themselves, everything changes. Congress writes the
laws and polices itself. Or doesn't, as the case may be.

The U.S. Constitution gives authority to the House and Senate individually to "determine the rules of its proceedings, punish

its members for disorderly behavior, and, with the concurrence of two thirds, expel a member."[11] Congress has taken this paragraph and run with it. A 2011 ethics report prepared for Congress begins by boldly stating that the House and Senate each have "sole authority to establish rules . . . punish and expel Members."[12]

They have legislated themselves as untouchable as a political class.

Members of Congress and their staffs are effectively considered exempt from many of the laws they define for the rest of us, and from executive-branch regulation. We ask our legislators to share power with the executive branch, and that means we do not let the latter rule over the former. Thus the Securities and Exchange Commission has a Division of Enforcement to go after private-sector insider trading (among other crimes), but the SEC cannot touch members of Congress. A former senior counsel with the SEC's Enforcement Division says of congressional insider trading, "It may be unethical, and it may be unseemly, but it's not illegal."[13] The four- and five-hundred-page House and Senate ethics manuals are silent on the matter of insider trading. The idea of using market-moving, inside-government information and trading stocks based on that information is simply not mentioned. (The senate manual does have an entire chapter on the use of the mail and Senate stationery for personal purposes, however.)[14]

The Senate *pretends* to take conflicts of interest seriously. When Senator Tom Coburn of Oklahoma was elected to the Senate in 2004, he asked to be able to continue to serve as a family physician, part time, on the side. The Senate Ethics Committee ruled that this would pose a conflict of interest and told him to shut his office down. God forbid we should have a senator making a little money as a doctor.[15]

The House ethics manual notes that there may be cases when legislation may affect the price of stock shares owned by a congressman, but adds that a member should not necessarily recuse himself from a vote, since by doing so he might be "denying a voice on the pending legislation."[16]

In other words, when a member of Congress trades stock based on information not yet shared with the public but revealed to him as part of congressional business, it is legal. It is even deemed "ethical." It can also be very, very lucrative.

Some economists argue that insider trading laws should be abolished. Professor Henry Manne, for example, makes this argument in his classic book *Insider Trading and the Stock Market.* Manne contends that insider trading gives corporate executives "positive incentives" to increase stock values. Whether you agree with Manne or not, however, not even he believes that such latitude should be extended to politicians. In an e-mail to the website Procon.org, Manne writes: "In my 1966 book I said unequivocally that insider trading by any government official on information received in the course of their work should be outlawed. We do not want them to receive extra compensation or outside compensation for doing their job. And, of course, all too frequently their access to this information is merely another form of a bribe, and that sure as hell is not legal."

In Manne's mind we have it exactly backward in our current laws: corporate executives can't do it, but politicians can.

In fact, politicians and their staffers not only can trade on inside information they passively receive, they can do the equivalent of an athlete betting on his own game. They can and regularly do introduce legislation and then buy or sell stock in companies that will be affected by that legislation.

"It is difficult to imagine a more obvious betrayal of the public trust," writes Andrew George, discussing this practice in the *Harvard Law and Policy Review*. "It is even more difficult to imagine that such behavior could be completely legal."[17] As Stephen Bainbridge, a law professor at UCLA, puts it, "Congressional insider trading creates perverse legislative incentives and opens the door to serious corruption. Yet, both Congress and the SEC have turned a blind eye."[18] Congresswoman Louise Slaughter adds, "Congress and the federal government are now so enmeshed in the operations of our financial markets that the potential for abuse by members of Congress, congressional staff and federal employees is staggering."

So are there any limits on this bad behavior by our lawmakers? If you ask a member of Congress, he or she will insist that financial disclosure requirements are sufficient. Politicians must disclose their financial transactions once a year for the previous year. In practice, however, as we have seen, it's nearly impossible to link their trades with contemporaneous legislative activity at such a distance. They can, and often do, file for extensions, meaning that their disclosures come, in some instances, eighteen months after they traded shares. Transactions are also reported in broad general ranges, making it difficult to establish volume price and profitability. Then there is the added problem that many politicians submit incomplete forms, obscuring either the dates or the amounts of their transactions.

Disclosure statements may actually encourage conflicts of interest and embolden politicians who believe that since they report a certain transaction, it becomes okay to do it. Indeed, several studies by behavioral economists demonstrate that disclosures may make things worse, by producing "perverse incentives": once politicians sign a form, they may believe they are free and clear to do what they want.[19]

• • •

So much for insider trading. What about broader conflicts of interest?

There are conflict-of-interest rules that apply to everyone in the executive and judicial branches of government, from the file clerk to the truck driver to judges to the secretary of defense. They are supposed to apply to the President too, and when it comes to personal finances, it does. But it is not illegal for a President to put fundraisers in charge of dispersing grants and loans to contributors and friends. Were a school superintendent to do this, he or she would be charged. But for a President? That's okay.

But these rules do not apply to legislators. They have their own. For the U.S. Senate, when it comes to raising conflict-of-interest concerns, the bar is set amazingly low: as long as a senator can prove that *at least one other person* besides himself benefits from a particular decision, he can pretty much use taxpayer money to enhance his own financial interests. The House rules are even worse. There is no such requirement.[20]

What this means on a practical level is that politicians can and often do use taxpayer money to help their own businesses and enhance the value of their own real estate. They can procure federal funds to develop a site where they own a sizable chunk of real estate. As long as it also benefits a neighbor, this is entirely acceptable. A member of Congress can secure federal transportation money and extend a light rail transit system right in front of her own commercial building and it is acceptable. Were a corporate executive to do this with corporate funds, she would more than likely be in trouble.

If you work anywhere in America—a corporation, the government, or the nonprofit sector—there are whistleblower laws to protect you if you report financial crimes. In 1989, federal ethics rules protected whistleblowers from retaliation if they exposed financial corruption in government. The Sarbanes-Oxley Act of

2002 extended those same protections to corporate America and nonprofit organizations. If you see your boss engaging in insider trading or fraud, you can report him to the authorities and you will be protected from retaliation. But Congress conveniently exempted itself from those requirements. Its members are effectively the only group of powerful people in America who can retaliate against whistleblowers who expose their financial crimes.

Another example: extortion, a crime defined as a person getting or attempting to get money, property, or services from someone through coercion. That coercion may include the threat to harm someone, physically or otherwise.

When ordinary Americans engage in extortion, they get arrested. Consider the case of a Bradenton, Florida, businessman who owned a tanning spa. One customer claimed that she was burned by his tanning lamps, and she sued him. The case was settled by his insurance company. The businessman was upset, however, and after the settlement he sent a letter to her two attorneys demanding $5,000 from them or else he would send complaint letters to local and state agencies, the state bar association, and the attorney general's office. The attorneys called the police. The businessman was arrested for attempting to "extort money" from the lawyers.[21]

Politicians have the power to extract wealth and favors based on their ability to help or harm people. While not as explicit as the extortion by the tanning spa owner, congressional extortion goes on regularly in Washington. When they want campaign contributions or preferential treatment, members of Congress may threaten businesses or individuals with harmful legislation. There is a name for this type of coercion: "juicer bills" or "milker bills," designed to "juice" and "milk" campaign contributions and favors from businesses and industries. Professor Fred McChesney, who teaches law at Northwestern University, says this is nothing short of "political extortion." Politicians threaten to tax something or regulate something in order to extract a campaign contribution, or even for personal financial gain.[22]

How powerful is this weapon? The mere threat of adverse legislation can affect a company's stock price. Two academics looked at thirty cases in which businesses were threatened with political action and the threats were later retracted. The study found that those threats "significantly" affected the stock prices of companies.[23]

Milker bills are often introduced in the area of taxes, says McChesney. Members of Congress threaten to impose a new tax and then withdraw the bill after campaign contributions flow in. Of course, the contributions were the point in the first place.

In the summer of 2006, Senate Majority Leader Harry Reid announced that he wanted a tax hike on hedge funds. At the time those funds were taxed at the capital gains rate of 15%. Reid declared that Democrats would put at the top of their agenda taxing hedge fund profits as regular income rather than as capital gains, meaning rates of 25% or higher. So they began working on legislation.

In late January 2007, shortly after the Democrats had captured both houses of Congress, Senator Charles Schumer sat down to dinner with a number of top hedge fund managers at Bottega del Vino in Manhattan. The net worth of the managers at the table totaled more than $100 billion. As the *New York Times* recounted, hedge funds up to this point had spent very little money on lobbying and campaign contributions. They were quite content to be left alone by Washington. But Schumer, who headed the Democratic Senatorial Campaign Committee, wanted to change that. And with

PAY UP, OR ELSE

Annual lobbying and campaign contributions by hedge funds

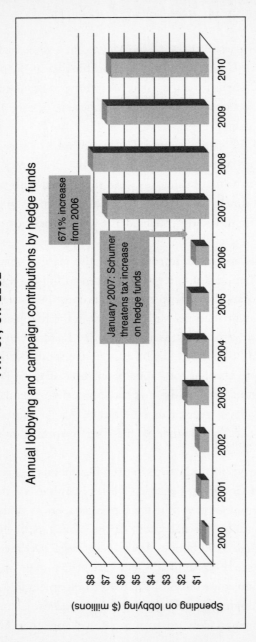

the threat of a tax increase, suddenly the hedge funds became very generous. According to the Federal Election Commission, over the course of the next eighteen months, hedge funds dumped nearly $12 million into campaign accounts—with 83% of the money going to Democrats. John Paulson, one of the most successful hedge fund managers, held fundraisers for the Democratic Senatorial Campaign Committee. James Simons, a hedge fund manager who made $1.7 billion in 2006 alone, donated $28,500 to the DSCC, and Schumer raked in $150,000 for his campaign chest. Bain Capital and Thomas H. Lee Partners, both Boston-based investment houses with hedge funds, gave generously to Senator John Kerry.

The political class also profited indirectly, because the hedge funds hired lobbyists, often the friends and former aides of politicians, to fight the bill. The Blackstone Group, which manages a huge hedge fund, had previously spent $250,000 a year on lobbying. Now Blackstone hired a number of Democratic Party lobbyists, including Schumer's former staff counsel, and spent more than $5 million on lobbying in 2007 alone. The Managed Funds Association, a lobbying group for hedge funds, also hired Democratic Party lobbyists, including a firm that employed Schumer's former aide for banking issues. Overall, dozens of former Democratic congressional staffers were hired with lucrative contracts to fight the bill.

Then, in the late fall of 2007, Senator Reid and his colleagues suddenly changed their tune. The Senate schedule, it seemed, was just too crowded to deal with the issue. The threat of a tax increase for hedge funds was withdrawn.

Politicians are so good at throwing their weight around that the banking industry had to lobby for legislation that would prohibit banks from lending to congressional candidates during election time. Why would they do that? Presumably out of fear that politicians would pressure them for special deals.

In our system of government, the legislative branch polices itself and the President is allowed to skirt conflict of interest laws because, well, he's the president. It is time for that to change.

9

WHY THIS MATTERS

Government is a trust, and the officers of the government are
trustees, and the both, the trust and the trustees, are created for
the benefit of the people.   — HENRY CLAY

THERE'S A STORY about a politician who returns from Washington to his home district to run for reelection. When his constituents learn that he is not yet a millionaire, they promptly vote him out of office. He *must* be stupid.

There seems to be only one sure-fire way to prevent the Permanent Political Class from getting drummed out of power: maintain extremely low standards. We have come to accept minor indiscretions, financial malfeasance, and profiteering on the taxpayer dime as regular occurrences. And as those indiscretions and crimes (for the rest of us) mount up and become more common, we become even more tolerant of them. The standards become lower still. To steal a phrase from the late Senator Daniel Patrick Moynihan (on a different subject), we have defined deviancy down in Washington. The quality of our leadership is so low because we expect so little.

The political class is able to exploit honest graft because they have been given a position of privilege and power, and they work very hard to persuade us that their well-being is necessary for our well-being. They work very hard to persuade us that they, and only they, are capable of "running" the country, or "managing" the economy. This, of course, is the classic appeal of the con: I may be a rogue, but I'm indispensable. George Washington Plunkitt made a similar appeal for Tammany Hall. Without the political machine in place, he warned, "it would mean chaos. It would be just like takin' a lot of dry-goods clerks and settin' them to run express trains."[1]

At the root of the Permanent Political Class is a profound sense of arrogance. A good military commander should never consider himself to be irreplaceable, but many politicians in Washington believe precisely that of themselves. It is an ugly form of elitism, less overt than what we would see from the royalty of Europe in the seventeenth and eighteenth centuries, when the Sun King could proclaim, "I am the state." The modern, subtler version of this arrogance is the politician's belief that if we restrict his ability to engage in legal graft, the nation will suffer, because we won't be able to attract bright people (like them!) to run the country.

Over the past forty years we have been governed by the best-educated political class in our history. Today, debts mount, the financial markets are in turmoil, the economy is in terrible shape—and the Washington games continue. The problem is not a lack of smart people in Washington. There is no "smart gap." There is, however, a "character gap." Like the financial crisis on Wall Street, the root of the problem is not ignorance but arrogance.

The Permanent Political Class tells us: We need them. Only

they can dissect the entrails of the latest bill or understand the complexities of financial reform. They are making so many sacrifices on our behalf, they say. They are smart and well educated and could be making a lot more money somewhere else, they claim. We should tolerate a little honest graft on the side, or the occasional financial indiscretion, like failing to report income on their tax returns.

Yet, of course, the political class is hardly the only group of people in the country making a sacrifice for public service. Our soldiers are underpaid. Those who enter West Point, the Air Force Academy, or Annapolis, or those who go through ROTC at a rigorous school, are just as smart. They certainly could be doing something else with their time. They choose the armed forces as an act of service; they are not looking to get rich as officers. Enlisted soldiers are not looking to cash in by joining the infantry. In the military they will never earn anything close to what they might earn in the private sector. And many of our best leaders over the last century or more have come out of our armed services. These are individuals who could have been running large corporations or institutions for far more money. Two-, three-, and four-star generals make less than a freshman member of Congress, even though they may be responsible for the safety and operation of more than 100,000 troops. If today we had a five-star general like Dwight Eisenhower—and we don't—he would still be paid less than a freshman congressman.[2] And yet it is impossible to imagine that the military brass would ever argue that they deserve to make a little "on the side" as indirect compensation for their service.

Indeed, in the early 1980s, when the United States was in the midst of another (smaller) budgetary crisis, President Ronald Reagan released to the public letters he had received from American soldiers serving in Europe. They weren't griping about possible cuts. Just the opposite: they offered to take a pay cut if it would help the country. When was the last time you heard a member of the Permanent Political Class offer to do that?

When Gordon England was appointed to become deputy secretary of defense in 2006, members of the Senate committee that would hold hearings and vote on his confirmation had a simple and blunt request: You must give up the lucrative stocks and options you have in companies that do business with the Pentagon. Such divestment had been a requirement of the Senate Armed Services Committee of senior Pentagon appointees for decades, designed to eliminate any "military-industrial complex" conflict-of-interest concerns that might arise. The restriction was not limited to just missile manufacturers or companies that made bullets. "We're not allowed to buy Coca-Cola stock because military guys drink Coke," said England, "and we couldn't have stock in cereal companies because military guys eat cereal."[3]

And who were the senators sitting across from England at those hearings? The same senators who wrote the defense bills, added earmarks, determined which military systems were bought or rejected. The same senators who were privy to private conversations with contractors and Pentagon officials, and received classified briefings on defense contracts, military systems, and Pentagon strategy. In other words, the very people who controlled the federal budget. They were free to buy and sell as many shares of defense stocks as they wanted to. Indeed, 19 of the 28 senators on that committee at the time held stock in companies that do business with the Pentagon.

The Permanent Political Class tells us they are concerned about financial corruption and financial crimes. They applaud legal crackdowns on corporate criminals and berate corporate executives for their huge salaries and tax shelters. The Permanent

Political Class believes that everyone needs to be policed on this front. Everyone, that is, except for themselves. Why did the Tammany Hall political machine gain so much power in New York City? Why was it a dominant force for more than a century? You could point to the patronage system, or the payoffs. But in the end the machine survived *because the public came to accept it.* New Yorkers came to tolerate the idea that you could use "legal graft" to get rich from "public service" because that was just the way things were done. Sadly, the same attitude holds true today when it comes to crony capitalism. We get outraged when members of Congress or the President breaks the law, but we ignore the legal graft that is far more prevalent.

As long as the Permanent Political Class gives us what we want, we are happy. This was precisely the goal of Tammany Hall: make people dependent on us. Plunkitt explained that the fondest dream of bosses like himself was a situation where "the people wouldn't have to bother about nothin'. Tammany would take care of everything for them in its nice quiet way."[4]

America is supposed to be a nation ruled by laws, not by men. Central to that idea of America is the notion that we are equal before the law. That means that the laws should apply equally to everyone.

For one of the chief architects of the Constitution, this notion of equality before the law was the "genius of the whole system." As James Madison wrote in *Federalist* No. 57: "I will add, as a fifth circumstance in the situation of the House of Representatives, restraining them from oppressive measures, that they can make no law which will not have its full operation on themselves and their friends, as well as on the great mass of society. This has always been deemed one of the strongest bonds by which human policy can connect the rulers and the people together. It creates between them that communion of interests and sympathy of sentiments, of which few governments have furnished examples; but without which every government degenerates into tyranny."

Why do the American people feel detached from Washington? Why are they fed up? Why do they feel little connection to their elected leaders? Why do our lawmakers in Washington seem to show so little urgency? Part of the answer lies in the fact that politicians are allowed to operate by a different set of rules. And that is a dangerous place for a representative government to find itself.

The Permanent Political Class is unresponsive to our concerns and needs because it is partly immune to the economic realities the rest of us face. Its business has, in a phrase popular with money managers, downside protection and guaranteed upside potential. For crony capitalists, there is a business cycle, but they control it and can make money no matter how and when it turns. This means socialism for the Permanent Political Class and its friends—and capitalism for the rest of us.

The Permanent Political Class offers all sorts of arguments to justify its special status and its exemption from conflict-of-interest and insider trading laws. Members of Congress will argue, for example, that they are required to disclose their financial transactions and assets, and voters can boot them out at the ballot box. Never mind that those financial disclosure forms are often filled out incompletely or incorrectly. According to the congressional newspaper *Roll Call*, 25% of them contain significant errors.[5] The point is, many lawmakers believe they must be kept above the fray, beyond the reach of the executive branch. They regularly exempt themselves from the level of scrutiny placed on other national leaders. They have even exempted themselves from Freedom of Information Act (FOIA) laws and open-document requirements. Their documents are as legally inaccessible as secret documents of the CIA—in fact, they are more difficult to obtain. At least some CIA documents become declassified and see the light of day. Congressional records never do. Congress passed the FOIA in 1966 because it believed that informed citizens would be better watchdogs. But Congress didn't want them looking into its own backyard.

Financial disclosure forms are required for elected state legislators, state judges, and county or city commissions around the country. But public officials are also required to abide by conflict-of-interest and insider trading laws and restrictions. If elected state judges, for example, were held only to the standards of federal lawmakers, they would be free to rule on cases in which they had a financial stake, as long as they faced reelection and filed financial statements. Would anyone like that idea?

In forty-five states, one or both state legislative bodies have a requirement that if a financial conflict of interest exists, a member legislator "shall not vote on the matter."[6]

American city councilors and county commissioners often have stricter rules than members of Congress, even though they have far less power and influence. In California, for instance, if you serve on a city council or county commission, you are subject to conflict-of-interest laws. As the state defines it, "You have a conflict of interest with regard to a particular government decision if it is sufficiently likely that the outcome of a decision will have an important impact on your economic interests." California has an oversight body, the Fair Political Practices Commission. One of the standards it uses is the "personal financial effect." If voting on a bill will cause you to gain or lose $250 or more in a twelve-month period, you should abstain.

The commission offers this hypothetical example: "The Arroyo City Council is considering widening the street in front of council member Smith's personal residence, which he solely owns. Council member Smith must disclose on the record that his home creates a conflict of interest preventing him from participating in the vote. He must leave the dais but can sit in the public area, speak on the matter as it applies to him and listen to the public discussion."[7] In other words, he can voice his opinion like any other citizen, but he cannot help make a ruling on the matter.

For members of Congress, not only are they allowed to vote in similar circumstances, they can also quietly insert an earmark into any big bill in order to widen the road in front of their house. As long as one other person lives on that road, the ethics committee will sign off on it.

Some people argue that members of Congress shouldn't be forced to comply with the same laws as the rest of us, because if they were, good candidates wouldn't run for office. Or that if they were required to recuse themselves, voters back in their districts would be disenfranchised. This is true, in the narrow sense that each recusal means certain voters' interests are not spoken for. But the grand claim of disenfranchisement should not be overused. Does anyone complain about disenfranchisement when a legislator skips a vote?

Members of Congress love to raise the banner of "separation of powers." When the FBI obtained a warrant to search Congressman William Jefferson's office in 2006, both Speaker of the House Dennis Hastert and Majority Leader Nancy Pelosi denounced the move as dangerous and unconstitutional. Jefferson was at the center of a fourteen-month investigation into charges that he accepted bribes. The FBI already had video evidence of Jefferson taking $100,000 in bribe money, and the Bureau found $90,000 in cash in his apartment freezer. But on Capitol Hill, the Permanent Political Class saw the raid as an outrage. Congressmen complained that FBI agents showed up at the Rayburn Office Building unannounced (imagine that!) and demanded that the Capitol Police let them into Jefferson's office immediately or they would "pick the office door lock." Some in Congress even threatened to retaliate by cutting the budget of the FBI and the Justice Department.[8] A federal judge dismissed these criticisms, arguing that Jefferson had turned his office into "a taxpayer-subsidized sanctuary for crime."[9] Of course, the judge was correct. It is understandable that members of the legislative branch would bristle at the use of coercive force by the executive branch against them, but not every example denotes a return to the civil wars of the British monarchy against Parliament.

Our legislators cling to the Speech or Debate Clause of the Constitution. Article 1, section 6 states that members of Congress "shall in all Cases, except Treason, Felony and Breach of the Peace, be privileged from Arrest during their Attendance at the Session of the respective Houses, and in going to and returning from the same; and for any Speech or Debate in either House, they shall not be questioned in any other Place."

That clause is not a get-out-of-jail-free pass for wrongdoers. It was designed as a safeguard against politically motivated legal action by the executive branch. British monarchs had used civil and criminal laws to block legislators who opposed the king. Who knew that over two hundred years later the legislative branch would use this as a shield against searches for criminal evidence?

If our elected representatives in Washington really want to cite the Constitution, they might begin with the Preamble: "We the People . . . ordain and establish this Constitution." We, the people of the United States, contractually grant Congress its rights. The Constitution is a contract between the people and the elected. When members of the Permanent Political Class use their public office for personal interest, they have breached that contract.

It was in the 1940s when the word "crony" was first applied to modern American politics. Arthur Krock, the famed *New York Times* reporter nicknamed "the dean of the Washington newsmen," used it to criticize the political machine–like methods of the Truman administration, and later applied it to others. Alluding to President Truman's former connections to the Kansas City political machine of Tom Pendergast, Krock wrote in 1946 that "the Missouri flavor is strong around the White House itself . . . and this has led to talk of government by crony." Harold Ickes, Truman's secretary of the interior, resigned from the administration in February of that year, saying, "I am against government by crony." Renowned journalist Walter Lippmann also used the term to criticize the Truman administration in a 1952 *New York Times* article, making reference to "the amount of politically entrenched bureaucracy that has earned for Mr. Truman's regime its sorry reputation for corruption, cronyism, extravagance, waste and confusion." After Truman retired from Washington, the word "cronyism" came up frequently in American politics — the Eisenhower, Kennedy, and Johnson administrations were all subject to charges of "influence peddling, conflict of interest, gift giving, and the like."[10]

We have seen waves of hearings, from Truman to Johnson to Nixon and so on, over scandals now mostly forgotten. Does anyone other than political junkies remember Abscam or the Keating Five? There have also been waves of reform efforts and rules changes, including the Ethics in Government Act (provoked by Watergate). Yet politicians continue to enrich themselves, their families, their friends, and their supporters through the practice of cronyism.

Montesquieu wrote in *The Spirit of the Laws*, "Commerce is the profession of equals." But not in an era of crony capitalism, where politicians increasingly call the shots and where better access is often more important than a better idea or better business plan. Business has often resembled a meritocracy: the entrepreneur with the best idea, the best product, the best business strategy, wins.

People vote with their purchases to select winners and losers. And investors looking to help a budding company will make their evaluation on the merits. Cronyism is the antithesis of a meritocracy.

Andrew Redleaf is the CEO of Whitebox Advisors, a highly regarded investment advisory service. Redleaf has had a long career running investment funds. He argues that crony capitalism isn't just unfair, it is a serious threat to our economic system, because "crony capitalists do not depend upon the general success of the economy to achieve their larger goals . . . The crony capitalist is instinctively satisfied with the notion of a zero-sum game, which, for his purposes, is better than a rising tide that lifts all boats. What good is it to the crony capitalist to see all boats lifted?"[11]

The crony-capitalist system is self-perpetuating. When they leave office, politicians become cronies of their former colleagues. Consider this simple statistic concerning the number of government bureaucrats and ex-politicians serving on corporate boards. In 1973, only 14% of Fortune 1000 companies had people with "government service experience" on their boards. By 1992, it had jumped to 39%. Since 2002, it has been over 50%. These numbers are even more stunning when you discover that during the same period the average number of outside directors on corporate boards has shrunk from 16 to 9.[12]

As one unnamed corporate executive put it, "We need someone on the board who is a veteran of the Washington scene, who knows and understands the people involved in the executive and legislative branches of the government, and who keeps an eye on what is going on in Washington. Somebody who has had Washington experience does make a great contribution to our board."[13] More and more, corporate leaders are coming to agree.

Researchers who have studied politicians and bureaucrats who retired and then joined corporate boards have found that government officials usually accept board seats within a month or two of leaving office. However, when a former government official's political party is out of power, "he or she [is] significantly less likely to gain a board appointment." In other words, this is about access, not about experience.[14] James Kristie, editor of the *Directors and Boards Journal* (yes, there is such a thing), says that ex-politicians on corporate boards are "very prevalent." What they offer is "knowledge of how government works, and access to a high-level network of leadership structure that many of the other board members do not." Sarah Teslik, executive director of the Council of Institutional Investors, notes that former politicians "have not brought any particular expertise that we can measure from the outside." She also finds that they are less likely to speak up at corporate board meetings and less likely to challenge CEOs than other directors.[15]

Ideally, the economy should be based on competition—companies competing for customers. But for many companies the "customer" that matters most is the government, and competing in Washington means political connections and access. The integrity of our markets is threatened when political influence trumps sound financial decisionmaking, and that is precisely what we face. A study that looked at the political connections of board members of S&P 500 companies found that the price of a stock rose an unusual amount following the announcement of the nomination of a politically connected individual to any given board of directors. In response to the Republican win in the 2000 presidential election, companies with connections to the Republican Party increased in value, and companies connected to the Democratic Party decreased in value.[16]

Another study by academics found that in the United States when powerful political figures died, companies to which they had strong connections saw their stock prices drop an average of 6% on news of their passing.

Journalist Ira Stoll conducted a more recent exercise centered around the first couple of years of the Obama presidency. He investigated the stock prices of corporations closely aligned with the administration — those whose CEOs were frequent guests at White House dinners or served on advisory boards. Was this hobnobbing a smart financial move? Did those connections help? Stoll writes:

> So I spent some time running the numbers. Suppose one began this strategy at the beginning of the Obama administration, buying one share of each publicly traded company with an executive appointed by the president on February 6, 2009 to the President's Economic Recovery Advisory Board. That would be UBS, GE, CAT, and ORCL. In the nearly two years since then (using the Monday February 7 closing prices, and using Yahoo! Finance historical price data that adjusts for splits and dividends), the gain would have been 145% — far outperforming the 52% return of the S&P 500 Index over the same period.
>
> Suppose that later that year, you decided to buy one share of each American publicly traded company that had a top executive attend President Obama's first state dinner at the White House, in honor of Prime Minister Singh of India. GE and CAT are on the list again, along with Honeywell, Pepsi (CEO Indra Nooyi) and Ethan Allen CEO Farooq Kathwari. The return through day's end February 7, 2011 would have been 46%, versus a 19% gain for the S&P 500 over the same period.
>
> Or suppose you wanted to invest in the publicly traded companies whose executives President Obama appointed on July 7, 2010 to the President's Export Council. Buying UPS, Boeing, Met Life, Disney, Pfizer, Dow Chemical, Ford, Verizon, United Airlines, ADM, and Xerox would have earned a 30% return over a period in which the S&P 500 gained 24%.[17]

There were exceptions, Stoll points out. Morgan Stanley, Bank of America, and UBS have underperformed the market. And Stoll's work has not undergone academic review (although I ran the numbers myself and came up with the same results). It could be a coincidence. It could be that President Obama surrounds himself with CEOs who help their firms consistently beat the market. But as we've seen, there is a body of research that shows this pattern has existed for quite some time. At what point do anecdotes start sounding more like epidemiology? When are coincidences so consistently aligned they appear to be predictable money trails?

It's no coincidence that the realm of crony capitalism is populated by billionaire financiers and large corporations. As the economist Will Wilkinson puts it, "The more power the government has to pick winners and losers, the more power rich people will have relative to poor people." And crony capitalism is the ultimate system of wealth redistribution: poor and middle-class taxpayers subsidize the superrich. Call it trickle-up economics.

It is the nature of crony capitalism to expand. Politicians want more campaign money and personal wealth, so they leverage their position and hand out favors. Corporations and financiers need those favors to get ahead, so they flock to Washington. If you can get early access to market-moving information, if you can secure government grants or subsidies or loans, if you can create regulation roadblocks for your competitors, why not? It is probably more cost-effective than developing a new product or service.

Crony capitalism also breeds inefficiency and confusion, blurring lines between the public and private sectors. The more complex the laws, the better it is for the Permanent Political Class and crony capitalists. A bloated bill of two thousand pages makes it easier to insert and hide things. For example, the massive health care reform bill included a provision, section 2711, that made it possible for certain entities to obtain waivers from the law. Did anyone outside the crony system understand the implications of that provision? The secretary of the Department of Health and Human

Services has granted more than a thousand waivers under section 2711. Many of these have gone to President Obama's political allies: labor unions and connected companies.

Had the health care bill been twelve pages long, it would have been a lot more difficult to hide the subject of waivers. Furthermore, a massive bill means more people hire lobbyists and experts to help them navigate it when it becomes a complex new law. A couple of years ago, *National Journal* analyzed the number of family members of sitting senators who were working as lobbyists. Fully thirty-three senators had family members who were registered as lobbyists or who worked for lobbying firms.[18] *That's one-third of the United States Senate.*

As Senator Tom Coburn of Oklahoma has put it: "Many legislators and their staffs have children or spouses who are or have been employed as lobbyists including many of the most powerful members and leaders of the Senate. Yet, no rules or laws currently prevent lawmakers or their staffs from being lobbied by relatives. Neither lawmakers nor lobbyists must report if they are related to each other."[19] Add to the list of laws and regulations that don't apply to Congress: rules against nepotism.

Dennis Hastert has a son who had been managing a record store in Illinois before Representative Hastert became Speaker of the House Hastert. When his father took the gavel, the son became a well-paid lobbyist in Washington. Senator Trent Lott's son, who was managing Domino's Pizza franchises before going to Washington, also made great money by becoming a lobbyist on the side.[20]

The rule of law, and the notion that no one is above the law, is fundamental to a healthy democracy. If we accept crony capitalism with a shrug and an eye roll, we might as well accept a world of bribery and out-and-out vote buying. Crony capitalism has a corrosive effect on our politics, our economy, and our character. And we don't have to accept it. It's one thing to say that our country was founded on the Constitution—as in "back then." It is another thing entirely to grasp that the Constitution is a living contract, rooted in legal soil that makes it wrong for politicians to serve themselves and their cronies. It is high time we did some weeding.

10

WHAT NEEDS TO BE DONE

The longer they live, the bigger babies they are.

— PROFESSOR WILLIAM GRAHAM SUMNER of Yale, 1895, on the demands
of businessmen and politicians for special privileges

L ET'S BE CLEAR: we need to stop coddling these people. Many others have been prosecuted for actions much less serious than those discussed in this book.

These people are not doing us a favor, and they don't deserve special treatment. There is no reason why only one place in the United States should be excluded from ethical standards and laws concerning insider trading, conflict of interest, nepotism, and cronyism. That in that same place, you won't be protected if you report financial corruption. After all, that may be the one place where we most need all these things: Washington, D.C.

The problem with Washington isn't gridlock. It isn't that

things aren't getting done. The problem is the corruption of the public spirit. The Permanent Political Class has no sense of urgency to change because, for them, business is good.

We need to break the cycle of crony capitalism, land deals, and insider trading. And we can do it simply by applying the rules that the politicians expect the rest of us to abide by.

As we have seen, disclosure requirements are not sufficient to stop cronyism. What about trusts? Many members of Congress put their assets in so-called blind trusts, and thereby appear to be above suspicion. Yet such trusts don't work either. Despite the name, blind trusts are far too often not, well, blind. And they are not dumb either. Senator Robert Toracelli had a blind trust, and by picking a political acolyte and longtime friend as his trustee, Toracelli made a killing on illegally manipulated stocks.[1] Senator Bill Frist had a blind trust where he held, among other things, shares of Hospital Corporation of America, a company started by his father. But that did not prevent the trust from making some well-timed stock sales, which set off an eighteen-month SEC investigation. Frist was cleared of all charges, but the episode highlighted the fact that a blind trust is not always blind. Politicians who have their assets in a blind trust whose trustees seem to show amazing deftness in predicting government actions need for serious scrutiny.

The rules of a blind trust are simple. You must select a trustee (it cannot be a family member) to direct the trust and deal with the investments. You cannot have a conversation with the trustee about the portfolio, and you cannot direct or suggest trades. Of course, what a politician can do is share nonpublic information, the kind that hedge funds pay a lot of money for, and then let the trustee make his own decision about how to react. As law professor Megan Ballard puts it, "The rules for these trusts do not include sufficient incentives to maintain blindness." Indeed, "blind trusts can mislead the public into believing that policymakers are avoiding conflicts, when they may not be doing so." As Ballard points out, the first elected U.S. official to use a blind trust was Lyndon Johnson, who was notorious for using his position to benefit his businesses. LBJ named two business associates and a family friend as his trustees. And he continued on as usual, with his trustees handling specific details.[2]

The simple fact is that politicians often select close colleagues, friends, and acolytes to run their blind trusts. Furthermore, once you establish a blind trust, according to the rules of the Senate, you are no longer required to disclose your assets annually, so it creates less transparency than before. Things that politicians are allowed to do in the dark are not always good.

Back in 1995, when legislators were arguing over the Congressional Accountability Act, which would subject Congress to federal antidiscrimination and other workforce protection laws, Senator Charles Grassley of Iowa said: "I hold the strong belief that we, in Congress, are merely representatives of the people. We are not better than the people we represent and we are not, by definition and determination, different from the people we represent. We are, as representative government intends, the people themselves."[3] It's time for Grassley's argument to be applied to crony capitalism on both Capitol Hill and in the White House.

Insider Trading

Henry Manne recognized in 1966 that "the federal government is the largest producer of information capable of having a substantial effect on stock-market prices."[4] The author of the standard text on insider trading knew Congress was a rich source of privileged information. What do our laws say on the matter?

When it comes to current SEC insider trading laws, there is a spirited debate going on among legal scholars as to whether current laws actually apply to Congress. Many contend that they don't, because our legislators are not fiduciaries (that is, client representatives) and are therefore not obligated to keep secret information secret. Other scholars argue that SEC laws on insider trading do apply to members of Congress. They claim it is illegal under Rule 10b-5 of the Securities Exchange Act, which is a general antifraud provision that prohibits deceptive conduct "in connection with" the purchase or sale of securities.[5]

But even if current laws do apply, the political reality is that the SEC is not going to enforce them against Congress. Remember, the SEC is funded by Congress. And SEC commissioners require Senate confirmation. Congress has oversight over the whole operation. Remember what happened when the FBI raided Congressman Jefferson's office? His colleagues threatened to cut funding for the Justice Department. And recall from the introduction how everything from IRS enforcement rates to listings under the Endangered Species Act are directly influenced by congressional power.

In Great Britain and throughout the European Union, it is already a crime to use insider government information for stock trades. Britain's Financial Services Act of 1986 extended the scope of the so-called Insider Dealing Act to explicitly cover all public servants. This included political or government information received "by all royal and civil servants and by all outside individuals receiving information from these servants." In other words, you better not pass the information and you better not trade on that information. This standard, if applied to the United States, would make clear to hedge funds that if they receive information from government employees and trade on it, they too may be liable.[6]

In 1989, the European Union deemed that insider trading laws for member states needed to meet a minimum floor. The EU said explicitly that insider trading meant trading on private information obtained "by virtue of the exercise of [one's] employment, profession, or duties." It specifically included "members of the central bank, the press, the parliament, the ministry of economics and of other institutions, committees and bodies who may possess inside information because of their profession or their duties."[7]

It would be difficult to apply the European standard here because in the United States there is no statutory definition of insider trading; it has been defined by our courts over time. I'm not one to adopt a law simply because some other country has it, but clearly the British and the Europeans are on to something: sensitive insider information means not just advance warning of a corporate announcement. It can also mean a key piece of legislation that will affect the stock price of a company. And if a legislator trades on this information, or shares it with someone else who trades on this information, he should face possible legal sanctions.

Conflict of Interest

The U.S. Supreme Court recognized decades ago "that an impairment of impartial judgment can occur in even the most well-meaning men when their personal economic interests are affected by the business they transact on behalf of the government."[8] All of us, if we are part of any sort of organized commercial enterprise, need to abide by conflict-of-interest laws.

As we've seen, this applies at the local, county, and state levels. Recently a city councilman in Sparks, Nevada, was censured by his state because he cast a vote in favor of a casino project that involved his campaign manager. He sued, claiming that he had a First Amendment right to vote on the matter. The Supreme Court, in a unanimous decision, denied his argument and found that conflict-of-interest laws were constitutional. Justice Antonin Scalia, writing for the court, said that conflict-of-interest rules "have been commonplace for over 200 years." He went on to note that when a public official votes, it "is not personal to the legislator but belongs to the people. The legislator has no personal right to it."[9]

Some states are going beyond simply censuring officials who have conflict-of-interest dealings. The State of Florida recently convened a statewide grand jury to consider how to deal with public corruption. Among its recommendations: "We also find voting conflicts of interest should be criminally punished . . . In essence, the law would tell public officials that they have a fiduciary duty to the public and that they must separate themselves from anything given to them while serving in this fiduciary duty. When a public official has a conflict, he or she should step aside and disclose the conflict. The only benefit the public official should receive is for the public, not for the public official or anyone else." Although Florida has not criminalized conflicts of interest, other states have.[10]

Land Deals

Why not apply to Congress the same ethical standards faced by members of county councils in most states? If they are asked to vote on a project that will benefit them directly, they must disclose that fact publicly and recuse themselves. Also, as a rule, a politician should not be a party to a land deal involving a campaign contributor. If someone has given an elected official more than $1,000 in campaign contributions, she should be barred from engaging in land deals with the donor.

Real Disclosure

The current financial disclosure forms required of politicians offer only a superficial look at finances and possible conflicts of interest. Here's an idea: make the House and Senate subject to the Freedom of Information Act. After all, Congress deemed it necessary that the executive branch be subject to the act. Even the CIA and the National Security Agency fall under its purview. Are congressional secrets more important to the safety and security of our nation? Such secrets are important only to the safety and security of our politicians. We should apply the Freedom of Information Act to Congress members and congressional committees.

Grants, Loans, and Insider Deals

As we have seen, when the federal government hands out billions of dollars in cash, there is often little transparency in the process. Corporations and nonprofit organizations keep records of major financial decisions. They also establish policies to protect against cronyism. When a compensation committee meets, for example, as a rule there can be no direct financial ties between any member and the company's CEO, and the committee must keep records of its votes and decisions. But at the federal level, when a $150 million guaranteed loan is offered, the process includes little transparency and no clearly established standards. Presidents should not be able to steer billions of dollars in taxpayer money to their friends, campaign fundraisers, and cronies, disguised as some so-called social good.

Breaking the Cycle of Crony Capitalism

Here are some initiatives that we must undertake to break the cycle of crony capitalism:

- Create a legal code that makes trading on nonpublic government information illegal both for those who pass the information and for those who trade on it. This is the standard in Europe, and it makes sense. But we need to be realistic and assume that the SEC will be a reluctant enforcer, so we will need to put additional checks in place.
- Corporate insiders trading their own company's stock are required to disclose these transactions to the SEC within two days. Why not apply the same standard to Congress? Members should disclose all transactions above, say, $5,000 within two days. The disclosure should be detailed, including the price and number of shares, and then placed online in a database. That will make potential insider trades easier to identify.
- Members of Congress should not be allowed to trade stock in companies that are overseen by their committees. If you sit on the Senate Banking Committee, for example, you should not be allowed to trade bank stocks. If you serve on the Senate Armed Services Committee, you should not be able to buy and sell defense stocks. Does your subcommittee deal with health issues? No pharma stock. This is the area where insider trading is most likely to occur, and where lawmakers are most

likely to obtain market-moving information from which they or their friends can profit.

- Apply whistleblower laws to Congress. If it's good enough for federal workers and corporate employees, it should be good enough for Congress. We should encourage congressional staffers, when they see financial irregularities like insider trading, to report them. But they will report them only if they know they will be protected from retaliation. They should be afforded that protection.

- Disallow "sweetheart" IPOs. One of the fastest ways for a member to make a quick buck is through an IPO. You can't legally hand a congressman $10,000 in cash, but you can arrange for him to participate in a lucrative IPO that is worth far more. "Special-friend" IPOs should be disallowed. Unless the initial public offering goes through a public auction, in which people can openly compete for shares in a bidding contest, members of Congress should not be allowed to participate.

- Review, revise, and enforce existing conflict-of-interest laws. Restricting stock trades based on committee assignments is a start, but not an end. Another possible way to avoid conflicts of interest would be for members either to abstain from voting when a conflict exists or to place their assets in mutual funds rather than individual stocks. Also, enforce the conflict-of-interest laws for senior White House officials and political appointees. Cronyism is cronyism, and political appointees should not be allowed to steer taxpayer money to former employees or business associates.

- Earmarks in which a member of Congress will receive a direct financial benefit should be disallowed, period. Taxpayer money should not be used as a resource to boost your property values.

- Family members of legislators should not be allowed to become lobbyists.
- Don't allow campaign contributions when Congress is in session. Twenty-eight states place restrictions on politicians receiving campaign contributions when the state legislature is in session. Extending this prohibition to Congress will make it harder for politicians to extort money from businesses.
- The federal government needs to get out of the business of offering grants and taxpayer-backed loans. It's a nice idea in theory, but in practice it's a disaster. The process is rife with corruption, favoritism, and cronyism. Don't let our lawmakers or political appointees in the executive branch pick winners and losers based on who their friends are. Today we have a form of socialism for the very poor and the very rich. It's unfair, and we can't afford it.

The problems we face today are not the result of the individual failings of a few leaders. What we face is a system that is compromised by the perception that U.S. public policy is a marketable commodity. It's time to fix it. Let's relegate the Government Rich to the ashbin of history. If you want to get rich, do it the legitimate way. Go out and produce a useful good or service that you have a right to sell.

NOTES

ACKNOWLEDGMENTS

INDEX

NOTES

INTRODUCTION: THE GOVERMENT RICH

1 Matthew Mosk, "Lawmakers Cashing In on Real Estate, Financial Reports Reveal," *Washington Post,* June 15, 2007.

2 Roger Scruton, "Politics as a Profession," *American Spectator,* October 2010.

3 Sean Wilentz, "Striving for Democracy," *Wilson Quarterly,* vol. 23, no. 2.

4 http://www.senate.gov/CRSReports/crs-publish.cfm?pid='*2%404P%5C%5B%3A%22%40%20%20%0A.

5 Andrew Biggs et al., "Are Taxpayers Getting Their Money's Worth? An Analysis of Congressional Compensation," Taxpayer Protection Alliance, July 2011.

6 Gabriel S. Lenz and Kevin Lim, "Getting Rich(er) in Office? Corruption and Wealth Accumulation in Congress," http://papers.ssrn.com/Sol3/papers.cfm?abstract_id=1450077, July 2009.

7 http://www.reuters.com/article/2008/03/13/us-usa-congress-wealth-idUSN1330776120080313.

8 http://chartingtheeconomy.com/?page_id=27.

9 http://www.cbsnews.com/stories/2009/02/12/national/main4798225.shtml.

10 Kevin Drawbaugh, "Get Elected to Congress and Get Rich: Study," Reuters, March 13, 2008.

11 Alan J. Ziobrowski et al., "Abnormal Returns from the Common Stock Investments of the U.S. Senate," *Journal of Financial and Quantitative Analysis*, vol. 39, no. 4, 2004, and Brad M. Barber and Terrance Odean, "Trading Is Hazardous to Your Wealth: The Common Stock Investment Performance of Individual Investors," *Journal of Finance*, April 2000, and Leslie A. Jeng, Andrew Metrick, and Richard Zeckhauser, "Estimating the Returns to Insider Trading: A Performance-Evaluation Perspective," *Review of Economics and Statistics*, May 2003.

12 Alan J. Ziobrowski et al., "Abnormal Returns from the Common Stock Investments of Members of the U.S. House of Representatives," *Business and Politics*, vol. 13, 2011.

13 Andrew Eggers and Jens Hainmueller, "Political Investing: The Common Stock Investments of Members of Congress, 2004–2007," http://www.gsb.stanford.edu/facseminars/events/political_economy/documents/pe_10_10_hainmueller.pdf.

14 http://www.bloomberg.com/news/2010-12-21/u-s-lawmakers-top-market-with-home-district-companies-stocks-study-says.html.

15 Jiekun Huang and Meng Gao, "Capitalizing on Capitol Hill: Informed Trading by Hedge Fund Managers," http://papers.ssrn.com/sol3/papers.cfm?abstract_id=1707181, April 18, 2011.

16 Ahmed Tahoun and Laurence Van Lent, "Personal Wealth Interests of Politicians and Government Intervention in the Economy: The Bailout of the U.S. Financial Sector," http://papers.ssrn.com/sol3/papers.cfm?abstract_id=1570219, December 31, 2010.

17 Gerald W. Scully, "Congressional Tenure: Myth and Reality," Public Choice, no. 83, 1995, and http://www.usatoday.com/news/washington/2009-01-05-new-congress_N.htm.

18 John P. Foley, ed., *The Jeffersonian Cyclopedia: A Comprehensive Collection of the Views of Thomas Jefferson, Classified and Arranged in Alphabetical Order* (New York: Funk and Wagnalls, 1900), p. 346.

19 Richard Painter, "Bailouts: An Essay on Conflicts of Interest in Ethics When Government Pays the Tab," *McGeorge Law Review*, vol. 41.

20 George Washington Plunkitt, *Plunkitt of Tammany Hall* (Gloucester, UK: Dodo Press, 2009), p 14.

21 Plunkitt, *Plunkitt of Tammany Hall*, p. 10.

22 Robert A. Caro, *The Years of Lyndon Johnson: Means of Ascent* (New York: Vintage, 1991), pp. 102–4.

23 Ziobrowski et al., "Abnormal Returns from the Common Stock Investments of the U.S. Senate," *Journal of Financial and Quantitative Analysis*, vol. 39, no. 4, December 2004, p. 662.

24 Thomas Peter Lantos, Financial Disclosure Statement, 2007, Schedule III—Assets and Unearned Income.

25 Timothy P. Carney, *The Big Ripoff: How Big Business and Big Government Steal Your Money* (New York: John Wiley and Sons, 2006), p. 79.

26 Carney, *The Big Ripoff*, pp. 80–81.

27 Daniel Michaels, "As Boeing Hits Turbulence, Uncle Sam Flies to Its Aid," *Wall Street Journal*, December 10, 2009.

28 William J. Hunter and Michael A. Nelson, "Tax Enforcement: A Public Choice Perspective," *Public Choice*, no. 82, 1995.

29 Maria C. Correia, "Political Connections, SEC Enforcement and Accounting Quality," Rock Center for Corporate Governance, Working Paper No. 61, July 2009.

30 Frank Yu and Xiaoyun Yu, "Corporate Lobbying and Fraud Detection," *Journal of Financial and Quantitative Analysis*, forthcoming.

31 R. Patrick Rawls and David N. Laband, "A Public Choice Analysis of Endangered Species Listings," *Public Choice*, no. 121, 2004.

32 John R. Gist and R. Carter Hill, "The Economics of Choice in the Allocation of Federal Grants: An Empirical Test," *Public Choice*, no. 36, 1981.

33 http://voices.washingtonpost.com/local-breaking-news/dc/7-of-10-richest-counties-in-dc.html.

1. THE DRUG TRADE

1 Tom Daschle and David Nather, *Getting It Done: How Obama and Congress Finally Broke the Stalemate to Make Way for Health Care Reform* (New York: Thomas Dunne Books, 2010), p. 11.

2 John Kerry, Financial Disclosure, 2011 and previous years.

3 http://www.nytimes.com/2009/08/06/health/policy/06insure.html.

4 John Kerry, Financial Disclosure, 2009, Schedule IV—Transactions.

5 Daschle and Nather, *Getting It Done*, pp. 178, 226.

6 Melissa L. Bean, Financial Disclosure, 2009.

7 Jared Polis, Financial Disclosure, 2009.

8 http://www.medicaltourismmag.com/newsletter/48/medical-tourism-expands-as-alternative-to-obamacare.html.

9 http://www.bridgehealthmedical.com/about-us/media-room/coverage/Company_cuts_medical_costs_by_sending_patients_to_US_hospitals_not_overseas.

10 Andrew Pollack, "Critics Say 12 Years Is Too Long to Protect Biotech Drugs from Generics," *New York Times* blog, Prescriptions: The Business of Health Care, October 15, 2009.

11 Richard Gayle, "Healthcare Reform Gave Biotech Everything It Wanted, and More," http://www.xconomy.com, March 24, 2010.

12 "Factbox: Winners, Losers, in House Healthcare Bill," Reuters, March 22, 2010, and Vanessa Fuhrmans, "Tax on High-End Health Plans Threatens Wider Group," *Wall Street Journal*, August 10, 2009.

13 http://query.nytimes.com/gst/fullpage.html?res=9400E5D91331F935 A25756C0A9619C8B63.

14 Johnny Isakson, Financial Disclosure, 2007, and Sheldon Whitehouse, Financial Disclosure, 2007.

15 James Sensenbrenner, Financial Disclosure, 2003.

16 James Oberstar, Financial Disclosure, 2003.

17 Jeb Bradley, Financial Disclosure, 2003.

18 John Kerry, Financial Disclosure, 2003.

19 John Kerry, Financial Disclosure, 2005, which reports on his capital gains for 2004.

20 John Kerry, Financial Disclosure, 2004, Part IV—Transactions.

21 John Kerry, Financial Disclosure, 2003.

22 Max Baucus, Financial Disclosure, 2010, Part IV—Transactions.

23 John Boehner, Financial Disclosure, 2009.

24 http://voices.washingtonpost.com/ezra-klein/2009/12/the_death_of_ the_public_option.html.

25 http://ipo.nasdaq.com/edgar_conv_html/2006/02/10/0000812796- 06-000010.html.

26 Jim McDermott, Financial Disclosure, 2004, 2005.

27 Amo Houghton, Financial Disclosure Statement, 2005, Addendum, stock transactions with Market Street Trust Company.

28 Amo Houghton, Financial Disclosure, 2003.

2. CRISIS FOR ALL, OPPORTUNITY FOR SOME

1 "President Bush Discusses Emergency Economic Stabilization Act of 2008," FDCH Regulatory Intelligence Database, October 3, 2008.

2 Spencer Bachus, "Confronting the Crisis," *National Mortgage News*, February 2, 2009.

3 Henry M. Paulson, Jr., *On the Brink: Inside the Race to Stop the Collapse of the Global Financial System* (New York: Business Plus, 2010), pp. 13, 153, 220, 296, 299.

4 The VIX is an index that measures the implied volatility of Standard and Poor's 500 index options. Between 1990 and September 2008, the VIX averaged 19. By the end of October 2008, at the height of the crisis, it reached a high of 89.

5 Bachus, "Confronting the Crisis."

6 "End of Illusions," *Economist*, July 17, 2008.

7 Paulson, *On the Brink*, p. 153.

8 Spencer Bachus, Financial Disclosure, 2009.

9 http://financialservices.house.gov/press/PRArticle.aspx?NewsID

=1684, and "FASB Delays Rule Affecting $10.5 Trillion in Bonds," *National Mortgage News*, August 21, 2008.

10 Paulson, *On the Brink*, p. 259.

11 Paulson, *On the Brink*, p. 260.

12 Paulson, *On the Brink*, p. 172.

13 Spencer Bachus, Financial Disclosure, 2009.

14 "Lead Financial Services Lawmaker Defends Trading," *USA Today*, September 23, 2008.

15 Paulson, *On the Brink*, p. 241.

16 James Moran, Financial Disclosure, 2009.

17 Shelley Capito, Financial Disclosure, 2008.

18 Richard Durbin, Financial Disclosure, 2009.

19 John Kerry, Financial Disclosure, 2008.

20 Rahm Emanuel, Financial Disclosure, 2003.

21 Alex J. Pollock, "GSE Reform on the Way," *National Mortgage News*, November 15, 2004.

22 http://www.washingtonpost.com/wp-dyn/content/article/2008/09/11/AR2008091102841.html, and Marc Hochstein, "U.S. Senator Is Urging Fannie, Freddie into the Subprime Market," *American Banker*, July 9, 1999.

23 John Kerry, Financial Disclosure, 2005.

24 Stephen Taub, "Global Blackout: Fannie Mae Freezes Employee Stock Sales," *Compliance Week*, May 24, 2005.

25 John Kerry, Financial Disclosure, 2006.

26 http://firstread.msnbc.msn.com/archive/2009/06/11/1962038.aspx.

3. IPOs: INVEST IN POLITICIANS OFTEN

1 Nancy Pelosi, Financial Disclosure, 2008.

2 "Visa Inc's $16 Billion IPO Oversubscribed, Analysts Say," MarketWatch.com, March 13, 2008.

3 National Retail Federation, nrf.com/swipefees.

4 "Fierce Fight Expected If Interchange Bill Reaches House Floor," *CardLine*, July 25, 2008.

5 "Congressmen Conyers and Cannon Introduce 'Credit Card Fair Fee Act,'" *CardLine*, July 18, 2008.

6 "And a Survey Says Most Americans Support the Act," *CardLine*, July 18, 2008.

7 "Fierce Fight Expected If Interchange Bill Reaches House Floor."

8 "Pelosi Statement on the House Passage of Expedited Card Reform for Consumers Act," http://pelosi.house.gov/news/press-releases/2009/11/releases-Nov09-card.shtml, November 4, 2009.

9 http://www.nacsonline.com/NACS/News/Daily/Pages/ND0526101. aspx.

10 http://washingtonexaminer.com/politics/2010/12/want-voice-wash-ington-invest-politician.

11 Christine B. Whelan and Tom Hamburger, "Lawmakers Joined Executives in Profiting from IPO Access," *Wall Street Journal*, September 6, 2002.

12 Benjamin Lesser and Greg B. Smith, "Rep. Ackerman Confirms He Introduced Israeli Officials to Defense Contractor Xenonics," *New York Daily News*, January 12, 2010.

13 Gary Ackerman, Financial Disclosure, 2005, 2006, and 2007.

14 http://articles.nydailynews.com/2010-01-11/news/17943510_1_alan-magerman-rep-gary-ackerman-annual-disclosure-forms.

15 Ian Talley, "Pelosi Investment Shows Unlikely Energy Alliance," *Wall Street Journal*, August 23, 2008.

16 http://seekingalpha.com/article/52737-this-week-s-energy-ipos-approach-resources-osg-america-quest-energy-partners-sandridge-energy.

17 Transcript, *Meet the Press*, August 24, 2008.

4. THIS LAND IS MY LAND

1 http://earmarks.omb.gov.

2 See Dennis Hastert's Personal Financial Disclosures, Kendall County Records, Doc. #200600025196, and Greg Hinz, "House Speaker Dennis Hastert Reaps Profit—and Controversy—Via Land Deal," *Crain's Chicago Business*, June 26, 2006.

3 http://www.sfweekly.com/2007-01-03/news/porkmistress-pelosi.

4 http://www.sfmta.com/cms/mcsp/cspover.htm.

5 "Public Transit Boosts Property Values, If Conditions Are Right," National Association of Realtors, http://realtor.org/transtools.

6 http://www.urbantools.org/policy-papers/transportation/light-rail-increases-land-value-a-california-case-study.

7 Matthew Mosk, "Lawmakers Cashing In on Real Estate, Financial Reports Reveal," *Washington Post*, June 15, 2007.

8 http://www.legistorm.com/earmarks/details/member/504/Rep_Bennie_Thompson_MS/sort/amount/type/desc/year/all/page/3.html, and http://www.opensecrets.org/politicians/earmarks.php?cid=n00003288.

9 http://www.countyofnapa.org/Pages/DepartmentContent.aspx?id=4294968331.

10 http://www.concordmonitor.com/article/226248/tallying-greggs-

earmarks-for-nh?CSAuthResp=%3Asession%3ACSUserId%7CCSG
roupId%3Aapproved%3ABA4A9537C4BF4594E11F4B09D8217743
&CSUserId=94&CSGroupId=1.

11 Judd Gregg, Financial Disclosure, 2001–2008.

12 Sharon Theimer, Associated Press, February 27, 2009.

13 Theimer, Associated Press.

14 Jamie Klatell, "Judd Gregg Joins Goldman Sachs," *The Hill*, May 27, 2011.

15 Christine Jindra, "Rep. David Hobson Steered Federal Money to Projects Near Properties He Owns," *Cleveland Plain Dealer*, http://cleveland.com/openers/2008/05/Sabrina_eatonthe_plain_dealer.html.

16 http://oig.tva.gov/PDF/09rpts/OIGMFinalReporttoEthicsComm.pdf.

17 Maurice Hinchey, Financial Disclosure, 2004–2008.

18 http://dailyfreeman.com/articles/2010/05/21/news/doc4bf60ccc73723880294024.txt.

19 Jeremiah Marquez, "Probe Targets Land Deal," *San Bernardino Sun*, September 6, 2006.

20 http://www.cnn.com/CNN/programs/anderson.cooper.360/blog/2007/07/earmark-request-hits-close-to-home.html.

21 Chuck Neubauer and Tom Hamburger, "Will the Pork Stop Here?" *Los Angeles Times*, November 13, 2006.

22 John Solomon and Kathleen Hennessey, "Reid Got $1 Million in Land Deal," Associated Press, October 11, 2006.

5. SPREADING THE WEALTH . . . TO BILLIONAIRES

1 Chuck Neubauer and Tom Hamburger, "Obama Donor Received State Grant," *Los Angeles Times*, April 27, 2008.

2 James Atkinson, "Smart Grid Grants: Not Currently Taxable, but There's a Hitch," SmartGridNews.com, March 12, 2010.

3 Bringing the Outside In, White House blog, http://www.whitehouse.gov, March 20, 2009.

4 https://lpo.energy.gov/?page_id=45.

5 "The Department of Energy's Loan Guarantee Program for Clean Energy Technologies," Audit Report, U.S. Department of Energy, Office of the Inspector General, Office of Audits and Inspections, March 2011, DOE/IG-0849, and Statement of Gregory H. Friedman, Inspector General, U.S. Department of Energy, Before the Subcommittee on Oversight and Investigations, Committee on Energy and Commerce, U.S. House of Representatives, March 17, 2011.

6 Briefing Memo, the White House, October 25, 2010, "Memorandum for the President, From: Carol Browner, Ron Klain, Larry Summers, Subject: Renewable Energy Loan Guarantees and Grants," pp. 1–8.

7 "First Solar Shares Rise on Government Loans News," Associated Press, May 12, 2011, and Duncan Greenberg and Tatian Seuffin, "The Next Billionaire Boom," Forbes.com, April 1, 2009.

8 Lindsay Riddell, "Stimulus Funds Spark Cleantech Projects, IPOs," *San Francisco Business Journal*, January 6, 2010.

9 Council of Economic Advisers, "The Economic Impact of the American Recovery and Reinvestment Act of 2009, Fifth Quarterly Report."

10 Leslie Wayne, "Democrats Look to Lobbyist to Finance Convention," *New York Times*, July 14, 2008.

11 To learn more about Mr. Westly's exploits, read the joint investigative report on him by the Center for Public Integrity and ABC News: Ronnie Greene and Matthew Mosk, "Green Bundler with the Golden Touch: Obama Fundraiser Got Clean Energy Aid, Then Perch to Advise Energy Secretary," March 30, 2011.

12 "It's Official: Solynara Is First Solar Company Awarded Federal Loan," *Wall Street Journal*, September 4, 2009, and "Obama's Kaiser Ties Criticized," *Tulsa World*, April 1, 2008.

13 Iris Kuo, "Solyndra and Government Support for Clean Tech Under Fire," Reuters.com, February 22, 2011.

14 Yuliya Chernova, "Loan was Solyndra's Undoing," *Wall Street Journal*, September 16, 2011.

15 Lucy Johnson et al., Synapse Energy Economics, April 13, 2010, and "Phase Out Federal Subisidies for Coal," Coal Utilization Research Council, Issue Brief: DOE Guaranteed Loan Program, January 2010.

16 http://www.recovery.gov/Transparency/RecipientReportedData/pages/RecipientProjectSummary508.aspx?AwardIdSur=75488&AwardType=Grants.

17 Lindsay Riddell, "Solar Trust Wins $2.1 Billion Loan Guarantee." *San Francisco Business Times*, April 18, 2011, and Paul Bedard, "Exxon, Chevron, BP Greased Obama's Campaign," *U.S. News & World Report*, March 14, 2011.

18 Todd Woody, "Reading the Fine Print of Brightsource's $250 Million IPO," Forbes.com, April 22, 2011.

19 Jim McTague, "Our Tough-Luck President," Barrons.com, July 10, 2010.

20 Robert Yoon, "Goldman Sachs Was Top Obama Donor," CNN.com, April 20, 2010.

21 http://wallstcheatsheet.com/trading/first-solar-shares-lead-todays-gains.html.

22 "Recovery Act Funds Support Geothermal Project Loan Guaranteed," Environmental News Service, February 28, 2011.

23 http://www.recovery.gov/Transparency/RecipientReportedData/
    pages/RecipientProjectSummary508.aspx?AwardIdSur=80623&Award
    Type=Grants.

24 Anne C. Mulkern, "Stimulus Cash Flowed to Completed, Under-Way
    Renewable Energy Projects," *New York Times,* October 19, 2010.

25 Mulkern, "Stimulus Cash Flowed to Completed, Under-Way Renew-
    able Energy Projects."

26 Kristen Lombardi and John Solomon, "Billions in Stimulus Money
    Given to Polluters," *Washington Post,* November 29, 2010.

27 Julie Rose, "Duke Energy Gives Democratic Convention Backing,"
    NPR.org, April 15, 2011.

28 Erika Lovely, "Obama Biggest Recipient of BP Cash," *Politico,* May 5,
    2010.

29 Mulkern, "Stimulus Cash Flowed to Completed, Under-Way Renew-
    able Energy Projects."

30 David Callahan, *Fortunes of Change: The Rise of the Liberal Rich and
    the Remaking of America* (New York: John Wiley and Sons, 2010), p.
    36.

31 Laura Litvan, "Emanuel Consults Buyout-Firm Allies in Debate Over
    Tax Increase," Bloomberg.com, July 26, 2007.

32 http://www.xconomy.com/seattle/2008/11/06/arch-co-founder-bob-
    nelsens-historic-close-up-with-president-elect-obama-and-the-tears-
    of-jesse-jackson.

33 http://www.businessinsider.com/meet-the-man-who-bought-jamie-
    dimons-house-michael-polsky-2010-9.

34 Greene and Mosk, "Green Bundler with the Golden Touch."

35 Greene and Mosk, "Green Bundler with the Golden Touch."

36 Michael Scherer, "How Fundraising Helped Shape Obama's Green
    Agenda," *Time,* March 15, 2010.

37 Dan Primack, "Amyris IPO: Which VC Backers Are (and Aren't) in the
    Black," CNNMoney.com, September 29, 2010.

38 http://english.unica.com.br/clipping/show.asp?cppCode=2757BCFA-
    ED51-44C5-8F0F-7C9C2E687D23.

39 http://www.telegraph.co.uk/earth/energy/6491195/Al-Gore-could-
    become-worlds-first-carbon-billionaire.html.

40 Jonathan Alter, *The Promise: President Obama, Year One* (New York: Si-
    mon and Schuster, 2010), p. 89.

41 Alter, *The Promise,* p. 60.

42 http://www.energy.gov/recovery/documents/RecoveryActCrop
    ped_24-34.pdf.

43 Paul Davidson, "Smart-Grid Standards an Issue in Economic Stimulus
    Bill," *USA Today,* February 4, 2009, and Alex Yu Zheng, "Stimulus Pack-
    age Will Create Winners in Smart Grid Standards," SmartGridNews.
    com, February 17, 2009.

44 Matthew Wald, "U.S. Backs Project to Produce Fuel from Corn Waste," *New York Times*, July 6, 2011.

45 http://www.cmo.com/leadership/conversation-cmo-year-finalist-wesley-bolsen-coskata-inc.

46 Steve Coll, "Crony Capitalism," *The New Yorker*, July 2, 2009.

6. WARREN BUFFETT: BAPTIST AND BOOTLEGGER

1 Andrew Clark, "Banking Crisis: Warren Buffett Sees US Bailout as a Golden Opportunity," *Guardian*, September 24, 2008.

2 http://www.bloomberg.com/news/2011-05-09/berkshire-will-record-1-25-billion-gain-on-goldman-redemption.html.

3 John McCormick, "Buffett Is Obama Meal Ticket," *Chicago Tribune*, August 16, 2007.

4 Ben Nelson, Financial Disclosure, 2008.

5 Jeff Zeleny, "Obama Sells Bailout Plan to Skeptics," *New York Times*, October 1, 2008.

6 "Buffett Calls Bailout Bill 'the Right Thing,'" *New York Times*, September 24, 2008.

7 Daniel Dombey et al., "U.S. Bill to Contain Payback Provision," *Financial Times*, September 29, 2008.

8 http://www.msnbc.msn.com/id/26976416/ns/business-us_business/t/warren-buffett-invests-billion-ge/#.TjhN1M033V0.

9 Charles Piller, "Bailout Helps Buffett Plenty," *Houston Chronicle*, April 4, 2009.

10 Daron Acemoglu et al., "The Value of Political Connections in the United States," Social Science Research Network, December 2010.

11 Ran Duchin and Denis Sosyura, "The Politics of Government Investment," Ross School of Business Working Paper No. 1127, University of Michigan, April 2011.

12 Robert Lenzner, "Calling Out Politically Connected Banks," Forbes.com, April 25, 2009.

13 Piller, "Bailout Helps Buffett Plenty."

14 Rolfe Winkler, "Buffett's Betrayal," blogs.reuters.com, August 4, 2009.

15 Piller, "Bailout Helps Buffett Plenty."

16 http://seekingalpha.com/article/100720-here-i-go-criticizing-warren-buffett.

17 Henry M. Paulson, Jr., *On the Brink: Inside the Race to Stop the Collapse of the Global Financial System* (New York: Business Plus, 2010).

18 http://blogs.wsj.com/deals/2011/04/21/warren-buffetts-profit-on-ge-investment-1-2-billion.

19 http://www.nytimes.com/2010/11/17/opinion/17buffett.html.

20 http://www.futureofcapitalism.com/2010/11/buffett-thanks-uncle-sam.

21 Andrew Frye, "Sokol Violated Berkshire Insider-Trading Rules, Audit Finds," Bloomberg.com, April 27, 2011.

22 Josh Mitchell, "Rail Deal Is Bet on Obama's Infrastructure, Climate Policies," *Wall Street Journal*, November 3, 2009.

23 Mitchell, "Rail Deal Is Bet on Obama's Infrastructure, Climate Policies."

24 See, for example, http://www.whitehouse.gov/the-press-office/2011/02/08/vice-president-biden-announces-six-year-plan-build-national-high-speed-r.

25 Matthew Lewis, "Buffett's New Company Sure Knows How to Lobby," Center for Public Integrity, November 6, 2009, and http://www.opensecrets.org/lobby/clientsum.php?id=D000021757&year=2009.

26 "Buffett's Obama Pigout," *New York Times*, August 25, 2011.

27 Steven Rattner, *Overhaul: An Insider's Account of the Obama Administration's Emergency Rescue of the Auto Industry* (Boston: Houghton Mifflin Harcourt, 2010), p. 102.

7. CRONIES ON PARADE: HEDGE FUNDS, DEFENSE CONTRACTORS, COLLEGES, BIG OIL . . . AND GEORGE SOROS

1 "Former US Secretary of State Offers New Hedge Fund Option," http://www.atrader.com.

2 Meng Gao and Jiekun Huang, "Capitalizing on Capitol Hill: Informed Trading by Hedge Fund Managers," Social Science Research Network, April 18, 2011.

3 Gao and Huang, "Capitalizing on Capitol Hill."

4 "Washington Whispers to Wall Street," Businessweek.com, December 26, 2005.

5 Brody Mullins, "Hedge Funds Use Lobbyists for Tips in Washington," Associated Press, December 8, 2006.

6 Mullins, "Hedge Funds Use Lobbyists for Tips in Washington."

7 Jessica Holzer, "Wall Street Goes Bargain Hunting in the Farm Bill," *The Hill*, April 23, 2008.

8 Joe Nocera, "From Pentagon, a Buy Rating on Contractors," *New York Times*, February 11, 2011.

9 "Did Steve Eisman Unduly Influence the Education Dept.?" CNNmoney.com, November 2, 2010, and Jim Angle, "Education Department Rules on For-Profit Schools Created with Investor's Help," Foxnews.com, May 31, 2011, and Andy Kroll, "Steve Eisman's Next Big

Short: For-Profit Colleges," Motherjones.com, May 27, 2010. E-mails concerning Eisman's meetings with Department of Education officials are available from CREW: http://crew.3cdn.net/37fff23ac9f0c849a8_vbsm6hbc5.pdf.

10 "Did Markets Know Obama Was Going to Tap Oil Reserve?" CNBC. com, July 6, 2011.

11 http://www.newyorker.com/reporting/2010/08/30/100830fa_fact_mayer.

12 http://www.nytimes.com/2010/08/29/opinion/29rich.html.

13 Richard Rahn, "You Lose, Soros Wins," *Washington Times*, October 24, 2008.

14 "Axis of Soros," *Wall Street Journal*, May 9, 2009.

15 Robert Kuttner, *A Presidency in Peril* (White River Junction, VT: Chelsea Green, 2010), p. 14.

16 Eamon Javers, "Soros, Gore among W.H. Visitors," *Politico*, October 31, 2009.

17 Louis Uchitelle, "Volcker Pushes for Reform, Regretting Past Silence," *New York Times*, July 11, 2010.

18 http://www.spiegel.de/international/business/0,1518,592268,00.html.

19 George Soros, "The Game Changer," *Financial Times*, January 28, 2009.

20 http://www.emc.com/leadership/tech-view/stimulating-ah-ha-phenomenon.htm.

21 http://www.teradata.com/t/industry-expertise/government.

22 http://4g-wirelessevolution.tmcnet.com/broadband-stimulus/topics/broadband-stimulus/articles/63191-extreme-networks-pushes-broadband-networks-into-rural-america.htm.

23 http://www.radware.com/Solutions/Enterprise/Industries/Government_US.aspx.

24 "Emerging Trends in Education Publishing," Cognizant.

25 http://www.nytimes.com/gwire/2009/06/12/12greenwire-doe-revives-futuregen-reversing-bush-era-decis-47303.html.

26 http://www.chron.com/disp/story.mpl/business/energy/6911328.html.

27 http://pseg.com/info/media/thought_leader/carbon_strategy.jsp.

28 General Electric Annual Report, 2008.

8. SOME ARE MORE EQUAL THAN OTHERS

1 Quoted in Edward Roeder, "Slippery Slopes: How Politicians Can Draw the 'Get Out of Jail Free' Card in the Game of Politics," *Campaigns and Elections*, August 2006.

2 Tony Mauro, "Recusal Report," *Legal Times*, October 10, 2008.

3 Kathleen Clark, "Regulating the Conflict of Interest of Government Officials," in Michael Davis and Andrew Stark, eds., *Conflict of Interest in the Professions* (New York: Oxford University Press, 2001), p. 53.

4 http://www.nytimes.com/2009/05/16/business/16insider.html.

5 See, for example, http://www.azauditor.gov/Reports/Counties/Yuma/SIU/SIU03-1.pdf.

6 Leonard J. Brooks, "Conflict of Interest in the Accounting Profession," in Davis and Stark, eds., *Conflict of Interest in the Professions*, p. 93.

7 http://www.nytco.com/press/ethics.html#B3.

8 Eleanor Randolph, "Guards of Press Troubled by SEC Suit," *Washington Post*, May 21, 1984.

9 U.S. Senator Ron Wyden, http://wyden.senate.gov/newsroom/press/release, July 15, 2010.

10 John Dorschner, "Senator Tells University of Miami He's Troubled over Hiring," *Miami Herald*, June 10, 2010.

11 U.S. Constitution, article 1, section 5.

12 Jacob R. Straus, "House Committee on Ethics: A Brief History of Its Evolution and Jurisdiction," Congressional Research Service Publication 7-5700, http://www.crs.gov.

13 Catharine Richert, "Public Citizen Gets It Right about Insider Trading Rules," Politifact, *St. Petersburg Times*, August 6, 2009.

14 Senate Ethics Manual, 2003, pp. 160–75.

15 Jeffrey Birnbaum, "Ethics Panel Finds Conflict with Senator's Job as Physician," *Washington Post*, April 6, 2005.

16 Committee on Standards of Official Conduct, 110th Congress, 2nd Session, House Ethics Manual, 2008 ed., pp. 234–37.

17 Andrew George, "Public (Self)-Service: Illegal Trading on Confidential Congressional Information," *Harvard Law and Policy Review*, vol. 2, 2008, p. 162.

18 Stephen M. Bainbridge, "Insider Trading Inside the Beltway," UCLA School of Law, Law-Econ Research Paper No. 10-08, June 30, 2010, http://ssrn.com/abstract=1633123.

19 Daylian M. Cain, George Loewenstein, and Don A. Moore, "Coming Clean but Playing Dirtier: The Shortcomings of Disclosure as a Solution to Conflicts of Interest," in Don A. Moore et al., eds., *Conflicts of Interest: Challenges and Solutions in Business, Law, Medicine, and Public Policy* (New York: Cambridge University Press, 2005), and Daylian M. Cain, George Loewenstein, and Don Moore, "The Dirt on Coming Clean: Perverse Effects of Disclosing Conflicts of Interest," *Journal of Legal Studies*, January 2005.

20 Clark, "Regulating the Conflict of Interest of Government Officials."

21 Beth Burger, "Businessman Dennis Kim Charged with Extortion," Bradenton.com, February 13, 2009.

22 Fred McChesney, *Money for Nothing: Politicians, Rent Extraction, and Political Extortion* (Cambridge: Harvard University Press, 1997).

23 R. Beck, C. Hoskins, and J. M. Connolly, "Rent Extraction Through Political Extortion: An Empirical Examination," *Journal of Legal Studies*, January 1992.

9. WHY THIS MATTERS

1   George Washington Plunkitt, *Plunkitt of Tammany Hall* (Boston: Bedford Books, 1993), p. 34.

2   http://money.cnn.com/2003/03/20/pf/saving/war_military_pay/table.html.

3   Scott Higham, Kimberly Kindy, and Dan Keating, "Senate Panel Ban Seen as Double Standard," *Washington Post*, December 19, 2010.

4   Plunkitt, *Plunkitt of Tammany Hall*, p. 42.

5   http://www.rollcall.com/issues/56_119/financial-disclosure-congress-205462-1.html.

6   National Conference of State Legislatures, "To Vote or Not to Vote: State Provisions on Conflicts of Interest and Voting," November 2009.

7   http://fppc.ca.gov/index.php?id=37.

8   http://www.washingtonpost.com/wp-dyn/content/article/2006/05/22/AR2006052201080.html.

9   "Judge Rules FBI Raid on Rep. Jefferson's Office Was Legal," Associated Press, Foxnews.com, July 10, 2006.

10 Joel S. Kahn and Francesco Formosa, "The Problem of 'Crony Capitalism': Modernity and the Encounter with the Perverse," *Thesis Eleven*, vol. 69, May 2002.

11 Andrew Redleaf and Richard Vigilante, *Panic: The Betrayal of Capitalism by Wall Street and Washington* (Minneapolis: Richard Vigilante Books, 2010).

12 Richard H. Lester et al., "Former Government Officials as Outside Directors: The Role of Human and Social Capital," *Academy of Management Journal*, vol. 51, no. 5, 2008.

13 Myles Mace, *Directors: Myth and Reality* (Boston: Harvard Business School Press, 1986), p. 86.

14 Lester et al., "Former Government Officials as Outside Directors."

15 *Market Call*, CNNfn, December 12, 2002.

16 Eitan Goldman, Jorg Rocholl, and Jongil So, "Do Politically Connected Boards Affect Firm Value?" *Review of Financial Studies*, vol. 22, no. 6, pp. 2331–60.

17 http://www.futureofcapitalism.com/2011/02/introducing-the-crony-capitalist-index.

18 Marisa Katz, "Family Ties," *National Journal*, March 31, 2007.
19 http://coburn.senate.gov/public/index.cfm?a=Files.Serve&File_id=f036d73d-7a10-4a57-a9ee-de3987049c31.
20 Carl Hulse, "In Capitol, Last Names Link Some Leaders to Lobbyists," *New York Times*, August 4, 2002.

10. WHAT NEEDS TO BE DONE

1 Tim Golden and David Kocieniewski, "Businessman Says Torricelli Arranged Stock Deal," *New York Times*, April 12, 2001, and Robert Ingrassia, "Old Pal Helped Torricelli; Probes Followed," *New York Daily News*, March 20, 2001.
2 Megan J. Ballard, "The Shortsightedness of Blind Trusts," *Kansas Law Review*, vol. 56, 2007.
3 Senator Charles Grassley and Jennifer Shaw Schmidt, "Practicing What We Preach: A Legislative History of Congressional Accountability," *Harvard Journal on Legislation*, vol. 35, 1988.
4 Henry G. Manne, *Insider Trading and the Stock Market* (New York: Free Press, 1966), p. 171.
5 Donna Nagy, "Insider Trading, Congressional Officials, and Duties of Entrustment," *Boston University Law Review*, vol. 91, 2011, p. 1105.
6 Bud Jerke, "Cashing In on Capitol Hill: Insider Trading and the Use of Political Intelligence for Profit," *University of Pennsylvania Law Review*, vol. 158, no. 5.
7 Jerke, "Cashing In on Capitol Hill."
8 *United States v. Mississippi Valley Generating Co.*, 364 U.S. 520, 549 (1960).
9 David G. Savage, "Supreme Court Upholds Conflict-of-Interest Laws," *Los Angeles Times*, June 14, 2011.
10 State of Florida Case No. SC 09-1910, Nineteenth Statewide Grand Jury, First Interim Report, "A Study in Public Corruption in Florida and Recommended Solutions," December 17, 2010, p. 43.

ACKNOWLEDGMENTS

The adventure that became this book started a couple of years ago when I first became enthralled with a simple but puzzling question: how is it that politicians enter office with relatively modest means and leave rich? Although I am responsible for the content of this book, I am thankful to the many colleagues and friends who offered guidance, assistance, and help along the way.

Let me say thanks to my good friend Stephen K. Bannon, who not only engaged intellectually with this project, but also challenged me to push further in explaining the deeper and broader problems of crony capitalism. Marc Thiessen, a good friend and partner in Oval Office Writers, offered helpful advice and moral support. Thanks is also due to Eric Singer of the Congressional Effect Fund in New York, who helped me refine my views and research concerning the interplay between congressional actions and American finance. Wynton Hall, as always, provided solid advice and sound input. I also greatly benefited from friends and colleagues who offered thoughts and comments, including Andrew

Breitbart, Larry Solov, Brian Baugus, Amy Ridenour, and Ron Robinson.

Bernadette and Owen Smith have been great friends and supporters going back more than a decade. I'm very thankful for their encouragement of this project, and I'm glad we are back in regular contact. I'm honored to be the William J. Casey Fellow at the Hoover Institution, and very grateful for it.

At the Hoover Institution, I appreciate the support and friendship of John Raisian, and of my colleagues, whom I see all too rarely. Bruce Nichols, my publisher, took a chance on this project, and I'm grateful that he saw the vision even more clearly than I did at the beginning. He not only kept me on schedule and corrected my errors, he offered tremendous advice on how to make the manuscript better. Bruce, it's an honor to work with you. My agents, Glen Hartley and Lynn Chu, are simply the best in the business. Period.

A project like this is, by its nature, a team effort. I was blessed to have the assistance of the following individuals who helped me enormously: Rhonda Adair for her editorial and intellectual input in shaping and completing the project; Tori Brooks for her research assistance; Seamus Bruner for his research work; Josh Eller for his research, input, and advice; David Healy Jr. for his research work and fact-checking; Tim Ward for his research work and fact-checking; Rick White, who provided expert advice and wisdom and consulted on this project in almost every aspect—conception, research, and writing; and Casey Wood, who provided research assistance and fact-checking support.

A special thanks goes to my assistant, Sally Jo Roorda, who put up with a horribly disorganized and messy office, a crowded schedule, and a neurotic boss, but still held everything together and did so with a smile.

Mom, you are the best. Maria, to whom this book is dedicated, your "little brother" appreciates you much more than he lets on. That needs to change.

My family—including my wife, Rochelle, and our children, Jack and Hannah (a.k.a. Sweet Pea)—has put up with a distracted man wandering around the house looking for books or documents for far too long. Thanks for being so patient . . . yet again.

INDEX